An Outlander's Journal

Essays on Country Life

೧൙

To Ken & Joyce Larue,
with thanks for reading
my column all those years.

Warm regards,
Eileen Graham
Oct. 18, 2009

An Outlander's Journal

Essays on Country Life

℘

By Eileen Graham

Word Association Publishers
www.wordassociation.com

Printed in the United States of America.

Cover Illustration by Margaret C. Brandt

ISBN: 978-1-59571-446-6
Library of Congress Control Number: 2009936828

Word Association Publishers
205 Fifth Avenue
Tarentum, Pennsylvania 15084
www.wordassociation.com

Acknowledgments

Each of the pieces in *An Outlander's Journal* has appeared in an earlier form as a column or essay in one or more of the following Pennsylvania newspapers: *The Gettysburg Times*, Gettysburg, the *Bedford Daily Gazette*, Bedford; the *Evening Sun*, Hanover; the *Standard-Observer*, Irwin; *The Gazette*, Indiana; *The Patriot-News*, Harrisburg; and in the *Herald-Mail*, Hagerstown, Maryland. One was published in *The New York Times*. I am deeply indebted to my editors at each of these publications.

For more than 25 years, I have worked to chronicle ways of life that have all but disappeared and to acknowledge the joys and sometimes harsh realities that accompany country living. I have selected items for inclusion in this book based on Adams County's singular people and places and my coming of middle age among them. Approximate times of original publication are noted, and each piece has been edited or updated to suit this format.

I am grateful for the wisdom and support of my friends Margaret Brandt, Dorothy Brown, Judy Carter, Teeta Daniels, Mary Hoffman, Michelle Simmons, Satsuki Swisher, Elizabeth Terry, and Bonnie Wachhaus.

For the love of my life, who brought me tea every morning, buried a forgotten hound on a mountainside, and has always been a good sport.

Contents

Prologue

Some places beckon to you; the best take root in your soul. More than 30 years ago, the undulating stretch of road that bisects the Peters Orchards north of York Springs, Pennsylvania, called me in just such a way. One blue-sky afternoon my husband, John, and I stopped at what was then a small fruit stand to buy apples, and I fell in love. Unfolding before us was a Grandma Moses crazy quilt embroidered with green knots of fruit trees and appliquéd with the faded planks of red barns and whitewashed Pennsylvania Dutch farmhouses. Solid, predictable, built and planted in hills that are the offspring of prehistoric cataclysms.

By the fall of 1974 we'd found one of those farmhouses for ourselves and moved our two boys and a dog named Pooch from the east shore of the Susquehanna River to a 21-acre farm just north of Gettysburg. While our new neighborhood was nothing like rural western Pennsylvania where John and I had grown up—most people back home voted Democrat and worked in a mill—the land bore some similarities, such as wild grapevines and a curled grass that prefers droughty soil, and I loved it for that. For the most part, my youth was spent in the rust belt's countryside where my mother bought 12 acres with $1,200 she'd inherited from her father. There were good times, but my stepfather, like some men in that geography, was an alcoholic and we lived for eight years in the foundation of a house that wouldn't be built until after I graduated from high school. I felt I didn't belong in a home filled with bickering or a neighborhood where men roosted on barstools while women cleaned up their messes at home. Much of my youth was spent in our woods, baring my outsider's soul to our collie dog, Laddie. I longed to belong, to fit in somewhere wholesome and safe. I graduated from college on loans, married my high school sweetheart and moved four hours away.

The Adams County acreage John and I chose after 10 years of marriage promised respectability, but the house and outbuildings needed work. Early on, I joked that we should hang out a shingle naming the place Falling-Down Farm. *Everything* was falling apart. Along with the quaintness for which Civil War-era places such as ours are known, we had bought a house with minimal plumbing and electricity, an antiquated heating system, no insulation other than potato sacks that had been stuffed between some of the studs, and a well that went dry a few weeks after we moved in. Work would be do-it-yourself as John's income allowed, since I had decided to stay home with the children, ages five and three. Progress was slow and dirty.

I was 32 when we moved, and unprepared for the isolation of our new life. On the eve of the U.S. bicentennial, the whole nation—especially our "Sixties" generation—romanticized America's agrarian roots. People we knew were homesteading in the country, restoring—god forbid you should *remodel*—old houses, eating natural foods, home canning summer produce, and making their own granola. That first winter was a long one. With family and friends now far away, the only people I saw regularly were door-to-door evangelists and vacuum sweeper salesmen.

John harvested our homegrown wheat, while I dried field corn under the grate of the wood stove and had it ground into nutty meal at an old-time grist mill. I baked bread from scratch, finding a catharsis in the physical act of punching and kneading the yeasty dough. We put out a huge garden, and I put by our good, clean food. In the midst of the 1970s oil embargo, runaway inflation, and a severe economic recession, every loyal American looked for ways to save energy. We eschewed the electric clothes dryer in all but the coldest months, turned off lights, and often cooked on the wood stove that also heated our home.

My finger joints throb just thinking about the paint scraping and sanding that were part of my daily *This Old House* routine, and those were the easy tasks. John shouldered the heavy loads, such as replacing beams in the house, digging fence postholes in rock, and muscling our submersible well-water pump 50 feet out of the ground when it went on the fritz, which was often.

I joined a group known as Homemakers and the parent-teacher organization at our elementary school where, as a former high school English teacher, I assumed my participation would be welcomed. It wasn't until I stood up at a meeting and questioned why we didn't have books in our library on other religions in addition to Christianity that I understood—I was an outsider.

I felt trapped, alone, depressed. Just as I feared I would never amount to anything but a laundress and "go-fer," I was asked by one of the county agricultural extension directors to drop by the office of the local newspaper and point out an inaccuracy in a recently published article.

After listening to my complaint, Jim Kalbaugh, then managing editor of *The Gettysburg Times* and a friend of my husband's, asked, "How would you like to work for us?" A part-time stringer position, covering municipal and school board meetings in our end of the county and reporting on them for ten cents a column inch, was open, he said, dangling the possibility of writing an occasional feature story in front of me like a shiny apple. I could work evenings, when John was available to watch the boys, and write from home, he said.

A door opened. I attended sometimes rowdy, mostly perfunctory township meetings, wrote them up and filed my stories. My beat was northern Adams County, and one of the first police calls I responded to involved a newborn drowned in a plastic trash bag at a farm pond near the one where our children swam. That case was never solved. People started recognizing me. "Are you Eileen Graham's husband?" they'd ask when they met John, and he'd smile and nod with growing pride. Before long, I was traveling around the county, interviewing interesting characters— they were *all* interesting to me—and fulfilling my high school ambition of becoming a journalist, albeit with a lot less pay than I'd imagined. Eventually, I gave up covering local events for a full-time stint, editing the newspaper's lifestyle section. But my first attempt at a job away from the farm required long hours and carried a load of guilt heavily weighted not just by our human children but by lambs, kids, and the occasional calf for which I was responsible. I walked away from the newspaper but felt hopelessly stuck, career on hold in paradise.

Then Kalbaugh asked me to write a weekly personal column.

I decided to try it and offered a month's work to start. It was the beginning of my 22-year relationship with a friend that existed only on paper, an opportunity to write about colorful people such as my neighbor, Hazel Johnson, who gardened by the signs of the moon, or to tackle in words situations that otherwise could have driven me over the edge. It opened a path into the hearts and lives of others. An unexpected gift had come my way wrapped in a weekly deadline.

In the meantime, I worked from home as a part-time farmer, freelance writer and public relations coordinator.

Seeking self-syndication for the column, I took day trips with stops at small and mid-sized newspapers. Miraculously, some good-natured editors agreed to a five-minute meeting when I showed up, unannounced with a handful of clips. A few, such as Ned Frear, whose family owned, edited and published *The Daily Gazette* in Bedford agreed to take my work on a trial basis.

At its peak, the column appeared in one Maryland and six Pennsylvania newspapers, yet by the time our sons were ready for college, my part-time work was contributing little to our family expenses. Eventually, I took a full-time job in higher education administration—first at Penn State's Mont Alto Campus and, later, at Dickinson College in Carlisle—though I continued to struggle with guilt about abandoning my responsibilities on the farm. Weekends, I wrote the column and never missed a deadline. In later years, my day job required a fair amount of travel, much of which I enjoyed, always knowing that, come Friday, I would once again return to the comforting landscape of my adopted home.

Adams County was then and continues to be unique: a geographic niche removed in time, charming of face with a magnanimous but sometimes dark heart beating just beneath its gently rolling green hills. From the perspective of my 60-plus years, I now look back and consider how different my life would have been somewhere else. I feel so deeply attached here that I sometimes wonder if there is any space at all left in my heart, for this place has made me who I am and I wouldn't change that for anything.

Eileen Graham

Chapter 1
Life in Genuine Stony Batter

ॐ

Geology: a science that deals with the history of the earth and its life especially as recorded in rocks [Merriam-Webster's Collegiate Dictionary, Eleventh Edition, Merriam-Webster, Inc., Springfield, Massahchusetts, 2008].

Geology figures large in Adams County, Pennsylvania, where, in the last century fruit trees learned how to thrive in rocky soil born just shy of a billion years ago during the Precambrian Era. Eons later—after the Atlantic had replaced the ancient *Iapetus* ocean that preceded it—people would stand atop the high rocky hills of northern Adams County to look south and observe the awful Battle of Gettysburg that marked a turning point in America's Civil War. In the human geology of our new home, I was to find treasure, though it wasn't readily evident on the stone-strewn surface.

We Bought the Stony Batter
May 1983

"Genuine Stones," announced the sign at the jewelry counter. I asked the clerk what kinds of stones they were. "I don't know, but they're genuine," she said. I chuckled as I walked away, thinking of the stones in Stony Batter. Of all the stones in the world, i.e., precious, semiprecious,

1

they have to be the most un-precious and yet most genuine in the universal characteristic of stones—hardness. A kidney stone is probably the only thing harder or meaner than a Stony Batter stone.

It wasn't until our second year on the farm that we discovered we owned most of the local Stony Batter. Not that we couldn't have guessed: our lawn, garden and fields were littered with stones. When we attempted to put in a fence for newly acquired livestock, we had to quarry the postholes. We mowed our lawn during the dry season and nearly set it afire with sparks that ignited when the mower blade bounced off stones growing in the yard. We plowed a plot for our garden and, with the soil, turned over wagonloads of the great flinty orange-colored gems.

"Save some for seed," our elderly neighbor Paul Bupp quipped when he saw us working to remove the rocks. By then we knew he needn't worry, for stone picking had become a perennial family affair, a rite of passage. "See how they do things together as a family," another neighbor remarked to his wife. Our boys cringed, knowing that every spring brought our most prolific crop as the frost squeezed a fresh harvest of boulders from the depths of the brick-red clay soil.

As I have heard the term *stony batter* in other Pennsylvania counties, it would seem that this is a generic designation applying to particularly stone-laden locales of various geologies. We soon learned that our Stony Batter stones are composed of ironstone, an igneous rock formed by ancient volcanoes that erupted here during the Jurassic Period. Ironstone closer to the surface seems to lie not in layers but in great piles of individual stones under the ground, constantly pushed to the top by the perpetual freezing and thawing movements of the earth.

Well drillers loathe the rock, which so annoyed old-time farmers that they used to dynamite immense boulders in their fields and haul the pieces off to the Stony Batter, where piles of them still lie. Habitually optimistic, the farmers performed their own spring rite of prying ironstones from their fields onto sleds made from the forks of trees and hauling them to a stone crusher that township officials operated on what is now our property during the years of the Great Depression. I learned these things from Harold C. "Bud" Miller, who worked for Huntington Township then and made 20 cents an hour tending the great jawed machine that cracked ironstone into four grades, from dust to cobblestones the size of a man's fist.

With typical Yankee ingenuity, they made do with what they had, filling potholes, "paving" dirt roads with cobbles spewed out by the crusher, and constructing fences with the big stones that were left in the fields. Since there was no shortage of building material, the farmers erected monumental fences, digging as far as three feet under the ground for footers and foundations and using the biggest stones to construct the fence bottoms and sides, which were then filled with smaller rocks and rubble.

Always, there was the hope of a blessing in disguise—a useful purpose for this abundant natural resource, the straw that might be spun into gold by some magical alchemy. During the years after the Civil War, prospectors staked claims in these hills, proposing to extract iron from the ironstone. In fact, it's said that in a quarry near here people actually mined iron ore that was smelted in a furnace at Idaville.

Since no ironstone barons are recorded in local history and no steel foundry has ever lit the skies of Idaville, it must be assumed that the only value of Stony Batter ironstone is in its constancy. Like other Adams County natives, it has always been here and always will be. Hard and enduring, it will never find its way to Tiffany's, but it is *genuine*.

3

Noel Potter, a retired Dickinson College geology professor, and his wife, Helen Delano, a geologist with the Pennsylvania Geological Survey, provided information for the recent editing of the previous piece and the introduction to the chapter.

Dickey's Hill
August 1983

Before TV and computers, before divorce court and psychological counseling, before the wheel and even before humankind, there was Dickey's Hill. Named for its turn-of-the-century owner, Richard "Dickey" Kline, Dickey's Hill is still there, jutting 1,116 feet above sea level into the air from the northeastern corner of Adams County. Within hiking distance from my house, it is where I go when I want to rise above my earthbound troubles.

On a clear day, you can almost see forever from the crest of Dickey's Hill. To the southwest, the church steeples of Gettysburg are visible. Southeast is Hanover, where lights blink on at dusk as if someone were illuminating an old-fashioned Christmas tree, candle by candle. And in between lies a patchwork of soft hills and fields, quilted with apple trees and cornfields, bordered by fence rows and woodlands, and knotted with houses, barns and silos.

Although nowadays children best know the view from this spot, old-timers remember what it was like when a climb up Dickey's Hill was a weekly family outing. "Most every Sunday evening we'd take a stroll up there," recalls Edith Bupp, Kline's daughter and heir to the promontory. "People used to walk up there on the Fourth of July to see the fireworks in Gettysburg."

In his youth, 69-year-old Harold C. "Bud" Miller took part in the annual ritual of hiking Dickey's Hill on the first balmy Sunday in spring to look for the sweet-smelling wildflower, trailing arbutus. "This attracted the young people," he tells me. "You'd go to church in the morning, and they'd say, 'Let's go and get arbutus.' " Teenagers started walking at one end of the neighborhood, picking up youngsters from other families along the way, "and before you'd know it there'd be 10 or 15 kids up there."

The girls pinned arbutus in their hair, which they wore pulled back in a knot or secured behind their ears with combs, he reminisces. "Those big white pines made a whispering sound in the woods—it was always a little windy in the spring—and you'd usually wind up with arbutus and a girl under one of those pine trees."

On one side of the hill is a place, Miller remembers, where pussy willows bloomed alongside a spring. "I'd go out there and lay down where the leaves would pile up in a little hollow. The birds would come, six or eight different varieties of them, and you could hear the wind blowing but it wouldn't [chill] you....Little things like that's what makes you remember Dickey's Hill."

Today the hill is a favorite camping spot for my children and other local youngsters who are imbued with the history of Dickey's Hill and like to recount the story of a Confederate soldier who was shot trying to steal horses in the Pine Swamp on the other side of the hill. His grave is said to lie just over the north side of the ridge, and some of them fantasize that the soldier still haunts the hill at night.

Long ago there were stories about the last Indian to inhabit the area, Bud Miller says. John Fitzgerald, who then lived at the foot of Dickey's Hill, told him and other youths about an old Indian squaw who lived at Pine Swamp until she died in the 1870s. "He said you could still see where the ground was piled up around her [lodge].

Stories also abounded concerning strange lights seen on the hill. The lights were called will o' the wisps or jack o' lanterns and were seen on damp nights in the fall when the earth was cooling off. "I've seen these close up with my brother," Miller attests. "First I was scared, but my brother said, 'It's a jack o' lantern.' It was luminous gas about three feet high, moving all the time. We just sat there and watched it, and then, just like that, it was gone. Then 100 yards down the creek bank it lit up again." The jack o' lanterns probably were luminous methane gas and the result of some chemical reaction occurring in the spring-filled area surrounding Dickey's Hill, Miller conjectures. They were observed until a drought in the early 1930s, he said. "I think that drained the water level so low that the chemical reaction couldn't occur."

Despite the local color, Dickey's Hill wasn't just a place of entertaining legend and good old days' remembrances; it was a place where people could go to look outside of themselves and put things in perspective. Even older people with canes and walking sticks would climb the steep slope to look out on their world. My neighbor Kenneth Bupp, one of Edith Bupp's sons and Dickey Kline's grandsons, recollects how he liked to look down and see his neighbors farming at the same time he worked the field near the top of Dickey's Hill with a team of horses. "That's when nobody had tractors, and I could see each one of them working, all with horses."

Marcia Showers, whose family owns land on part of the hill says, "Every fall, we love to take a hike up there just when the leaves are turning."

Whatever the season, it's hard for things to look bad from Dickey's Hill. The six o'clock news, personal problems and tomorrow's hectic schedule all seem small when I get to the top. The view isn't just breathtaking—it's enlightening. Dickey's Hill always has been there and always will be. From it, you can—as the lyrics from the musical, *On a Clear Day*, advise—"rise and look around you." And on a clear day you really can "see who you are."

When Haley's Comet became visible from most of the northern hemisphere in 1986, we went up to Dickey's Hill to view it one clear, starry night. Kenneth Bupp, now in his eighties, still farms his grandfather's land.

White Lambs and a Purple Cow
September 1983

"Look at that dear little thing," and "Oh, so soft," passersby remarked, fingertips testing the nap of carded wool on our son's 4-H project as he prepared it for showing at the county fair.

"Could my daughter have her picture taken with that cute little lamb?" asked one woman. "It's a lot of work, isn't it?" another observed. I smiled, biting my tongue and suppressing the *if you only knew* response in my mind. "Here, let me show you my scars!" I wanted to yell before they moved along to the next stall. "See this finger? Almost had that amputated giving worm pills to lambs last month...And this gimpy foot? That's where one of the mothers got me at hoof-trimming time." I couldn't show her the bruises that had made me the brunt of a ram's head butt.

"What's his name?" inquired another admirer. "Bandit," I replied, silencing the urge to add, "and most appropriate, too. That little bugger robbed me of an elderberry pie." It would have taken too long to tell her about my unfulfilled summer dreams.

At the beginning of every season, I make a mental list of things I plan to do. This summer, baking elderberry

7

pies topped the list. I watched low marshy areas in the spring, marking the locations of elder bushes when they bloomed so I might return to pick their stems of blue-black fruit just in time to enter a prize-winning pie in the county fair. But this year, when the berries ripened, there were other things to do.

Our 12-year-old son informed us that, to compete well, market lambs must be sheared and groomed. Sheep shearers are a rare breed and don't come out for just one or two sheep. Since all the flocks in our area had been clipped much earlier in the summer, we would have to shear the lambs ourselves or take them somewhere to be shorn. A friend and fellow 4-H mother knew of a shearer in a nearby town, so she and I planned to pack our boys' market lambs into my pickup truck and visit him. What we hadn't planned was a breakdown of the truck.

There was no alternative but to pile lambs and all of our four kids into the back of her vintage station wagon with a tailgate that wouldn't open. Children and lambs clambered in over the back seat, serenading us with maas and baas in soprano, bass and tenor. They didn't even mind a detour we encountered at sidewalk-sales days in town. We were just another part of the show: a traveling circus in a maroon '63 Ford that looked like a purple cow. City folks, strolling by as we stopped at a traffic light, pointed and laughed. "Did you see that?" one teen yelled to his buddies. "It's a bunch a sheep in that old station wagon," chortled another.

We followed sketchy directions and finally found the shearer's farm—sans the shearer. Mark Gutshall was taking in a second cutting of hay and had to be hailed from a nearby field by his mother. The purple cow lumbered across a gully and up a steep bank to a barn where we waited for him in the summer heat, thirsty kids and sheep hanging out the windows.

"Guess what, ma," one of the kids announced, "there's a pig in there havin' babies." He pointed to an adjacent shed where a mountainous old sow was indeed delivering piglets. A radio played easy-listening music to calm her in her solitary activity.

Eventually the lambs' short fleeces were shorn between wagonloads of hay as we shuttled sheep from car to barn and back to car again, and the traveling circus was finally on the road home. Later, we would clean the animals with buckets and water, currycombs and cards. The Ford would be cleaned as well, but despite buckets of Pine Sol, it would always smell sheep-ish.

Cicadas hummed their hurry-up, hurry-up refrains as summer melted into a series of hay bales, water buckets and grain. We learned to administer injections, vaccinating the animals against a host of maladies, including overeating disease or *enterotoxaemia*, to which lambs are particularly vulnerable. We fenced new pastures, walking every inch to weed out toxic plants. We penned the lambs in one day and the next they escaped, defoliating azaleas, rhododendrons and hollies—all supposedly poisonous to sheep. We gave them lush green hay, and they ate brambles and straw.

For reputedly shy, cooperative animals, they had always been full of surprises, beginning with the birth of our first set of twins on a bitterly windy early spring night, two weeks ahead of schedule. One new mother stubbornly decided she didn't want the job when her lamb was born. We rolled her on her side every few hours so he could nurse and took advantage of the time to snuggle the soft, curly-fleeced baby. June and July dried up and slipped away along with the elderberries, and before we knew it August was upon us.

"Maybe next year," I thought as another fairgoer peeked over the sheep stall, smiled and walked on. Across the way in the beef barn, parents were helping their children to groom hulking steers. Ears were daubed, short-haired coats scrubbed, and hooves dabbed with shoe polish. Kids and grownups nervously paced, examining their animals. "Now that's a lot of elderberry pie," I said aloud to myself and hurried to ringside for the show.

The purple cow died and Mark Gutshall began traveling to our farmettes as the Graham and Wachhaus flocks grew from one to three or four ewes each and a ram or two. When he married, Mark brought his wife and, later, their two little girls to experience our spring shearings.

Just a Pond
January 1984

It could be any pond at the bottom of any hill, along any back road, anywhere USA.

It's there only because the land wasn't good enough for anything else. Too wet to cultivate, not long ago it was a bottomland pasture for horses. Now it's a year-round rural resort for its owner and a half-dozen neighborhood adolescents, who hike off the path of video voodoo to poke around its banks, perennially watching and waiting. Waiting for the first real freeze of winter when autumn hoarfrost in a nearby meadow turns to ice-palace glass and the waxed-paper skin on the pond becomes a frozen slab many inches thick. The splintery dock that shimmered in its summer reflection now is rooted to granite-hard feet. There they sit to put extra socks and hand-me-down skates on dangling kid-feet as soon as the owner judges the ice safe.

They all show up that first rock-cold day as if summoned by some silent messenger no less mysterious than the one that calls birds and butterflies south. Red-cheeked with wonder, they watch and listen for the shotgun snap of weather cracks. They skate and slide on feet, bellies and bottoms, using twigs for hockey sticks, a crumpled Coke can for their puck, and bearded bulrushes as a goal.

The fat bass that coolly ignored their hooks in summertime now dozes beneath, dreaming sugarplum frog-egg fantasies. He is careless of the warmth on top, as a game of Crack the Whip puts one big boy at the lead, stringing the other kids out in a whirring frenzy till the littlest one skids on knees and elbows from the end of the tail.

Winter freezes and thaws the pond's heavy blanket till it seems worn out, waiting for spring.

Finally, gray rain melts it and the pond becomes a chirping, cheeping nursery for tadpoles, dragonflies, crickets and snakes. Sunlight turns the stiff bones of last year's goldenrod to compost for marsh grass and dandelions. And they watch again with tackle boxes and coffee-can night crawlers for the grandfather bass to appear.

"I saw the big one!" comes a wide-eyed cry.

"Over there, he is. That's him fer sure!" yells another.

School ends, and they watch and wait for that first mild day of June when the water has warmed to a friendly temperature and they may shed shoes and socks, jeans and sweatshirts, splashing and shivering in celebration of another grand opening of the old swimmin' hole.

The owner watches, too.

"Always afraid someone might get hurt," he cautions, wary of the threat all waters possess. And the kids learn, hanging over the edge of the tired old dock, watching as big fish eat the minnows and turtles eat the fish.

Summer yawns, and the pond is a giant bathtub where they whoop and holler and cannonball off the side, upsetting the balance of nature with one fell swoop of an

11

inner tube and countless consecutive belly whoppers.

On crystalline nights they camp on a neighboring hillside. Listening for crickets and bullfrogs, they sleep five or more pups in a two-man pup tent with sleeping bags spilling into the crabgrass and a dirty tube sock holding a flashlight to a bent aluminum center pole. When they sleep out under the stars, they sometimes wake to find deer jumping over their sleeping bags.

School starts. September sighs. And the pond becomes a looking glass, clear to the bottom and still at last. Ready to bed down for another winter of watching and waiting.

It's just a pond, any pond—a watering hole for birds and animals and tadpoles of every species.

Dick Miller's pond is quiet now that our boys and their contemporaries are grown and mostly gone from the neighborhood. Not long before he died, Dick told me how much he missed those young, playful voices.

Secrets, Signs of Seeds
May 1985

My neighbor Hazel Johnson is a keeper of old-time seeds. She has jars and tins full of them.

Seeds for flat, crisp Italian beans. Seeds for lima or string beans, both bush and climbers. Every size, shape and color—jet-black, blue speckled, green, yellow, mauve, brown, and brown speckled—they're the makings of a magic beanstalk that would eat Jack's heart out. Among them are "four kinds of beans I brought here 20 years ago," she says, alluding to her residence on the old Spangler place.

Pepper seeds, pimento seeds, and tomato seeds. No flamboyant hybridized Early Wonders or Better Boys, these are simply named "Green," Red," or "Big Pink."

There is dill. "You can save that, you know," she tells me. And there are tiny seeds for turnips: "Last year it was a picture out here. Did you ever see them goin' to seed? They're *bee-you-tee-full!*" Hazel's pronunciation puts diamonds and emeralds on this word.

And, of course, salsify, "oyster plant," seeds in a tall old Maxwell House coffee jar. "I don't know how long I've had that." She shakes her head, explaining that salsify roots are best left in the ground over winter and dug in spring to make mock oyster stew. "And you do it the same way. Cook it, and dress it with butter and milk."

There's no secret to keeping the old seeds going, she says: all it takes is collecting the pods, shelling them out, and saving the best. "My mother, she always saved seed—anything that got dry." Hazel, too, has been saving seeds for most of her 73 years. "I try to put some in every year just so they won't die out."

For as long as I've known her, Hazel has been planting the same variety of red potatoes, saved since the days before certified seeds. Certified seed potatoes, she tells me, are like most hybridized seeds: "You can plant them again one year. But after that, they go back, and all you got is tiny little balls." These red potatoes are sweeter than the usual white Kennebecs or Katahdins, she says. "And they make the best fried potatoes." Her neighbor once planted just one and dug 17 potatoes from a single stalk.

But potatoes, like everything else in Hazel Johnson's loamy garden, are always planted and harvested according to "the signs." She fetches a current copy of *Baer's Agricultural Almanac* hung in her kitchen on a string threaded through the pages and complains that it no longer has a hole for hanging: "Every year they're cuttin' down...it's getting' less and less." Root crops are best

13

planted under astrological signs that pertain to the lower half of the body, she explains, showing me the almanac diagram of man's body as governed by the twelve zodiac constellations or signs. Above-ground plants are best sown under signs governing the top half of the body.

"Lima beans is something the sign really talks to. You plant them in Virgo and you'll get all flowers," she warns. Gemini, the twins, is a barren sign, not good for planting anything, she says. "Now what you can do then, is you can stir weeds.

"I like fish (Pisces) and Cancer." Pisces is a watery sign that helps anything planted under it to resist drought. Cancer is both watery and fruitful and most favored of the signs for planting.

"What surprises me is from day to day how [the planting climate] changes," she tells me, setting out two glasses of a cool, ruby-colored liquid. Home-canned raspberry shrub she learned to make from her mother. "You have to watch the moon signs, too, for some things." Symbols for phases of the moon, these often appear on calendars along with the astrological signs and can be found in the almanac.

For example, anything planted in Hazel's "upgoing" phase, when the moon is farthest south and turning back north—the crescent moon is shown resting with its back on the ground like a cradle—will get very tall. One year, she declares, her snap peas, planted "in the upgoin'" had vines so high, "you had to get a ladder to pick 'em." However, she cautions, spinach or lettuce planted in the up sign will go to seed in a hurry. Hazel believes other things also show the moon's influence. "You watch. Shingles on a house will turn up on the ends in the upgoin'. I had an old board out here in the garden, and if the moon was in the upgoin', that old board was just like a rockin' chair."

At the ready in one raised bed is a spading fork she

uses, just like her mother, to turn the soil every spring. And around back is the woodpile where she stacks logs she's chopped to the right size for the cookstove that warms her house in winter.

Hazel's silver-white hair and clear blue eyes shine in the sun as she shows me where the peas she planted already are climbing one side of a wire fence. Small pansies, "monkey faces," she's saved for years bloom nearby. Like them, she is perennially "'in the upgoin'.'"

On several occasions I sampled Hazel's raspberry shrub, which she used as a summer cooler and said gives one "the most soothingest feeling." The recipe is as follows:

Cover raspberries—several quarts at least—with cider vinegar; let stand overnight, roughly 12 hours, in a large, acid-proof container such as an enameled pot or a gallon crock. Cook the raspberries and vinegar, bring to a boil and simmer till soft. Then strain through a jelly bag or clean cloth. Add sugar to taste. Pour the hot liquid in jars and seal. Modern canning techniques advise putting such products in an additional boiling water bath for approximately 30 minutes.

When the jars are opened, an equal amount or more of water should be added to the ruby vinegar. Serve in a glass full of ice cubes on a hot afternoon.

Mighty Oak
November 1985

It was on a gray autumn day that the Bupps cut the great oak in their woods near my house. The trunk of it—as wide around its middle as I was tall—lay in the stub-

15

ble of a cornfield, trimmed of its gnarly roots as if these farmer-loggers had given a pedicure to a mastodon they'd dug up while planting winter wheat.

"It was time," Edith Bupp, then in her late seventies, had said when I wondered about the cutting of the old oak and the loss of a local landmark. The tree had lived a good long life, she told me, but it was ailing. It was time for it to go, now before it got too sick to harvest.

Edith was my neighbor, the matriarch of a native family whose farms surrounded our newly acquired acreage on nearly every side. She and her family had welcomed us to these parts with invitations to their annual hog butcherings, apple butter cookings and cider pressings. One of the first features I published locally was a story about syrup the Bupps cooked from the sap of maples in their hollow.

Edith and I didn't agree about some things. She didn't hold much with book learning, never permitted her kin to do any kind of work on Sundays, and wouldn't have an automatic dishwasher in her house on a bet.

But we both liked flowers. In my garden came to bloom the same varieties that grew along her lane and next to her picket-fenced kitchen garden: hardy narcissus and daffodils she called Easter flowers, jonquils, old-time woods hyacinths with a fragrance mail-order nurseries have yet to duplicate, half-wild Oriental poppies she justly warned me would "take over," and sweet balsam, an annual that somehow blossomed every year.

It was a give-and-take relationship: mainly, she gave and I took.

She talked and I listened, dozing in the broad-armed wooden rocking chair that sat near the cookstove in her kitchen. There was always a blue and white checked damask tablecloth covering the staples of bread, butter and homemade jelly on the table where she served a large cooked dinner every day at noon for the menfolk.

Edith was short and round with her white hair pulled back in a knot at her neck. In later years she limped on the leg that was to give her so much trouble. I never saw her without an apron except on rare occasions when she left the house to go visiting. She could have been any little old lady in these parts. But she wasn't.

Edith and her husband, Paul, lived by choice with few modern conveniences in much the same way people had lived 50 years earlier. They'd had eight children on the farm where she was born. She was aware that they were something of a local legend and offered lore to anyone who asked—her contribution to provincial learning.

From her I learned to dry field corn and take it to a nearby mill for grinding into yellow meal that tasted of summer sun all winter. I learned to mash peaches and apricots into a fruit leather Edith's mother was making a century before Betty Crocker got the notion to promote plastic-textured imitations. And I learned to look out on the world from Dickey's Hill, the highest spot in the county.

Dickey's Hill belonged to Edith Bupp and she was proud of it. It was named for and bequeathed to her by her father, Dickey Kline, who worked it with a team of horses. Her sons still farm it. At the crest of Dickey's Hill is a swath of woods; as legend has it, a Civil War soldier is buried there and still haunts the area. At its bottom lies a small farm pond where every summer pink lotus lilies bloom next to rusting farm machinery, as unexpected as silk kimonos rustling among the cornstalks or mastodon feet resting in the cornfield.

It was on a gray autumn day that Edith died. I saw the cars and trucks heading back her lane and wondered if the visit I'd postponed for so long would be too late.

Her obituary was duly printed in the newspaper. It told where she went to church and listed the names of her husband and all her children and the numbers of the grandchildren and great-grandchildren. But it didn't mention the jonquils in the lane, the rocking chair in the kitchen or the blue-and-white damask cloth on the table. It didn't tell about Dickey's Hill and the lotus lilies.

It didn't say that a great oak in the neighborhood had fallen.

Well into her seventies, Edith's daughter Lucille still keeps her mother's kitchen garden going. Edith's jonquils and poppies bloom in my yard every spring.

Maundy Thursday House Blessings
March 1988

I tried selling *The New York Times* on this story, but they thought it was a big yolk. It's no laughing matter, however, that folks hereabouts are preparing to throw eggs over their houses three days before Easter.

No, it isn't some crazy trick. It's a serious tradition. A tradition rediscovered by a friend of mine who is, shall we say, somewhat egg-centric. Every year at this time my friend—a regular person with a regular job, a dog, husband and kids—gets ready for Easter by throwing eggs over people's houses and planting them.

"Sure," you say.

I'm here to tell you that the egg lands intact, is buried at that very spot and, according to tradition, brings good luck to the house for the following year.

If at all possible, eggs laid on Maundy or Holy Thursday, the day before Good Friday, should be used. For, according to Germanic folklore, a Maundy Thursday egg has special powers and when thrown over a house or barn will ward off lightning and evil spirits, protecting all within its trajectory.

My friend has access to Maundy Thursday eggs from

a neighbor whose chickens are now laying 18 eggs a day in celebration of spring. And after years of practice, she has a loyal following of true believers. "It won't work for skeptics," she says, noting that doubters invariably end up with a smashed egg. And a good arm helps, especially when farmhouses with steeply pitched roofs are to be blessed. Originally, it was old-world peasants with thatch-roofed cottages who did this, not Pennsylvania farmers with two and three stories under a tin roof.

But it works. For five years, I've watched Maundy Thursday eggs sail over my precariously high slate roof, bounce off the grass in my front yard, and settle on a patch of green, remarkably unscrambled and gloriously uncracked.

In the early days, according to author Venetia Newall, eggs were imbued with the spirit of fertility; the practice of burying them, probably pagan in origin, is shared even with the Chinese. When Christianity moved into Europe, the egg tradition was assigned to Holy Thursday, then called Green Thursday, signifying renewal of the earth and the return of life after the darkness of winter.

Modern people who practice the egg-over-the-house tradition in our locale have included a parish priest, whose farmer-parishioner gives him Maundy Thursday eggs when he comes to offer communion, and a Lutheran minister whose wife claims the fertility rite worked in reverse for her last winter when she neglected the custom. "I didn't have any more children," she sighs with relief, "though we did acquire one more cat."

My friend's 17-year-old son, who was 12 when he started lobbing eggs over his parents' rambling farmhouse, seems to have fared well. This year he was a high school basketball star.

Last year was the first in more than ten Easters, however, that my friend failed to make her appointed Maundy

Thursday rounds. There had been years when the list of homes to be blessed was so long that her family pitched over farmhouses, ranch houses and bungalows well into the night. Then, too, there was the Holy Thursday when they had to make multiple throws over one house because a German shepherd was catching the eggs in midair. And the time when they instructed a fellow who'd had surgery, lost his mother, and suffered a mild stroke, all during the previous year, to stand on the front porch.

All those years, we egg-throwing folk managed to hang onto our roofs and maintain reasonably good luck. But last year was different. At Easter, my friend's family took a trip to Texas. No Thursday eggs were gathered to bounce benevolently in our yards and be planted on the spot.

What followed was a universally awful bad year. Kids got sick, roofs leaked, dogs died, and grownups fell into malaise. "I can laugh about it now," says one unconsecrated convert: "Last year my husband left me."

Believe me, this year we're all lining up. New Yorkers may not hold with this stuff, but we country folks know—when it comes to blessing a house, a little yolk comes in handy.

I think I first met Bonnie Wachhaus on the Adams County Public Library's bookmobile, where one day she found a book, An Egg at Easter: A Folklore Study *by Venetia Newall, that gave her the idea for re-creating the previously noted tradition.*

Haymaking
July 1989

"Make hay while the sun shines," goes the old saw. But this summer the sun didn't shine so much in June, so our haymaking was postponed till July. Past its prime, our orchard grass had long ago gone to seed—even the timothy and red clover were old—but we made hay.

There's a furor about making hay. When the fields are cut, all other activity stops and the rest of the world exists in limbo; there may be bloodbaths in China or earthquakes in Peru, but none of it matters until the hay is in. It's an event, a tradition among country dwellers and, if we're not careful, a modern sort of shibboleth for us outlanders.

I tried explaining it once to a city friend who wondered why I wouldn't attend her party on a summer Saturday. "Can't. Tomorrow we make hay," I offered. Vexed, she gave me a "you gotta be crazy" stare.

I'd asked myself the same question a dozen ways, a dozen other summers. Why would anyone want to sweat and cough and itch and ache? Of course, the primary motivation is necessity: once frost hits the summer pastures, there is nothing for our sheep and goats to eat without a store of hay. Still, we could buy it; lots of so-called part-time farmers do. But it wouldn't be the same. There would be no watching for groundhog holes under the hay rake flails, no urgency to beat afternoon thunderstorms, no feeling of satisfaction when the barn is finally full.

Someone surely would deliver foreign hay to our door, maybe even stack it in our hayloft for a price. But it wouldn't be our hay, grown on our ground, under our sun. For my husband there would be no reason to bounce along in the saddle of the old Ferguson; for me, no opportunity to ride the creaking wooden hay wagon. Often, I've thought some composer should write a haymaking symphony similar to Aaron Copeland's ballet, *Appalachian Spring,* celebrating the harmony of man and grass and mechanical beast.

Hay balers are expensive, cantankerous contraptions, and for that reason we don't own one. This year our neighbors, the Bupps, baled our several acres with their New

Holland baler and kicker. Swallowing windrows of fodder, compacting and binding them with twine to the rhythm of a one-cylinder gasoline engine, a kick baler is a remarkable invention when it works, eliminating the catching, stacking and sweating required with non-kicking balers. When we first moved to the farm, bale catching was my job. Soon our sons were old enough to help, and I had little more to do than make iced tea and scoot bales to the elevator. The new position was okay by me, for I remembered falling overboard on a hay wagon when I was a child.

Some unexpected things do find their way into our bales. Rocks are a common impurity, followed by aluminum cans and plastic bags. Every now and then we come across half a snake. One winter my husband found his long-lost Timex watch, still ticking, in a bale he was feeding to the sheep.

Worst of the haymaking jobs is stacking in the barn, my husband's domain. Bales roll off the elevator's motorized conveyor belt faster than the stacker can blink. Sweat rolls off his face and chest, and hayseeds prick his eyes and ears in the rarefied atmosphere of the hayloft, where the temperature sometimes hits 100 degrees. Sun streams through cracks in the plank siding, illuminating a million floating dust motes while the stacker eats, breathes and sneezes hay dust until every last bale is crisscrossed into an architectural mass and the barn is filled with the fragrance of drying timothy.

This year we had fewer bales than in times past. But the smell of them lingered just as sweetly. As always, the field across the way lay clipped like chartreuse velvet. And our hay fleshed out the bones of the hayloft for winter.

"It's a good feeling," sighed my husband. "We'll have enough for another year."

*With no more livestock, our haymaking days are
over. I deeply miss the smell of new-mown hay, but
the birds, butterflies, groundhogs, rabbits, box turtles and an occasional red fox seem grateful that
our former hayfield has now grown into a meadow.*

Gargol Was on the Map
May 1990

Outsiders don't believe there's a place called Gargol
on the map. Gargol is north of Gardners, about a mile and
a half due east of Idaville and just a short distance from
my house. There's nothing along the road to mark it—no
sign that says, "Welcome to Gargol," no village gathering
place. In fact, nobody I know remembers how it got its
name. But long ago it was the site of a post office and, con-
sequently, I think, earned a spot on the Pennsylvania
map. That was before Nellie Riley's parents, Gertie and
Webster Guise, bought it and operated Guise's Cash Store
on the corner.

Nellie is my neighbor. She moved from the old house
next door to an apartment in town some years ago, but
she still is my neighbor and always will be. Back in the
1930s, she and her husband rented the house where I live
now, and four of their children were born here in what
they called "the front room."

She showed me a picture of the building at Gargol that
housed the post office, then Meals's Store, and finally
Guise's Cash Store.

"It had fourteen rooms, that house," she said—one
large room upstairs was used as a hall—and that didn't
count two finished rooms in the attic. The picture shows
her long-skirted mother and her two brothers standing
next to several hitching posts in front of the big wooden
house; it was taken by an itinerant photographer in 1915,

she thinks. Nellie was just a baby then.

"Do you know why most of the windows are shuttered?" she asked.

Looking at the vintage sepia photo, I could almost taste the summer heat. "To keep the sun out?" I guessed. The shutters were painted a dark color, and the house and surrounding picket fence appeared to be white.

"See those big windows in front? My mother always had dishpans hanging in them—to advertise," Nellie offered. Outside the three windows, horse collars hung. Her mother ran the store, and her father farmed their forty acres.

A pair of double doors at the corner opened into a large room lined with shelves full of pots and pans, metal buckets, men's work clothes, shoes and dry goods. "My mother had two 9 X 12 Brussels rugs in front," she boasted. The dry goods came in on the train at Gardners Station, and Blaine Beamer, who hauled things between Gardners and York Springs in a horse-drawn wagon, delivered them to the store.

"And we sold all kinds of groceries.... People brought their eggs in for mother to sell, and butter (Gertie churned her own butter) and, of course, baking soda." Sugar and coffee beans were measured out by the pound. Baking soda was sold in a one-pound tin because back then people baked biscuits almost every day for breakfast. "She had her regular customers that bought a lot of baking powder...and you'd get a dish with it—Hall China. I still have some of that china and I wouldn't give it up for nothing."

A big stove heated the store, and near it sat a cracker barrel filled with round water crackers. Cheese came in a round box then, and customers often bought a nickel's worth of cheese and some crackers, which they would eat as they sat and talked.

"They'd come in, evenings, and loaf," Nellie laughed. Drummers also stopped by to market their wares to Mrs.

Guise. Spittoons at strategic locations added tobacco juice to the ambience of the place.

"We finally got an ice cream cabinet. It was Newman's ice cream, and they packed it in ice. And when I was older, my mom and dad said if I kept the cabinet clean, I could keep what I made from it. Ice cream came in big, high tins that held five gallons. Three of them fit in the cabinet, and you had nickel cones and dime cones." These days, Nellie says, she gives her grandson a dollar for an ice cream cone, "and he comes back and says, 'Grandma, I'm short.'"

After a while, folks started going to larger stores in nearby York Springs, and Nellie's parents quit the business when she was just ten years old. The big old shuttered house burned down in 1967.

A new house sits on the corner where Guise's Cash Store once did business. But Gargol is still on the map.

I'm sad to say, Gargol no longer appears on Pennsylvania's state map, though it still was listed in 1990.

Lillich's Feed Mill
February 1991

Not much has changed since Charlie Gembe bought Lillich's Feed Mill in York Springs. You can still buy sacks of White Lily flour and cornmeal there, along with sugar cure for home-cured hams and bacons if you're so inclined. They'll still leave a bag of feed on the loading dock for you to pick up after hours.

Charlie wasn't there the Saturday we went in to have our grain ground, but his assistant, Mike Rothenhoefer, was. A few things have changed since he came here in '82, Mike said. What with the government buyout of dairy herds and the retirement of some older farmers, less and less of the business is dairy-related these days. More and more, it's grinding of horse feed.

Small-timers with weekday jobs make up the Saturday morning trade at the mill nowadays. It wasn't always that way for me. I remember calls I made first thing on a February morning when I woke up to a calf with diarrhea (the scours) or a lamb rejected by its mother. My husband had the workaday job, and I stayed home with my typewriter, the sheep and our kids.

"You got any Lamb Manna Charlie?" Charlie worked for Lillich's then.

"Yup, one sack here. I'll put it out for ya."

You still back in to offload your grain into a pit with a shiny auger that carries it to the grinder. This Saturday two boys about eight and nine years old, waiting for their father whose grain was already in the mixer, stood mesmerized by the noise of the grinder as we shoveled our yellow kernels of summer into the pit. Freckle-faced, they stared as each orange cob vibrated toward the corkscrew mouth at the bottom, eventually to be pulverized and spat out at the other end.

Mike stuck a chew of Red Man into his cheek as the man and his boys drove off in their overloaded pickup, and it was our turn.

"Alpha-Lyme makes any feed a better feed," it said on the side of the mixer where our grain went after being fed into the hammermill and the weight bin. By Mike's calculation, we had 600 pounds of corn. To it he added 60 pounds of soybean meal, 10 pounds of minerals and six pounds of salt—yellow, red and white—and the big conical-shaped mixer with its belts and pulleys metered it into our grain so that every pound contained the same percentage as the other.

We returned a pile of burlap sacks today for credit, and after the remaining bags were filled each was tied with a piece of twine cut from a thick rope of hemp.

The miller's knot is a curiosity, according to Mike, who looped the twine over his fourth finger and wrapped it twice around the top; it's a knot that won't come loose no matter how hard you pull. "I get a kick out of some of the customers. You show them every time they come in here, and they still don't know how to tie it. But then they're not tying a bag a minute every day."

Out here the worn hardwood floorboards are polished to a shiny patina by the dust. A feed mill *is* dust. Dust draped on long graceful cobwebs swooping from the rafters. Dust on the windows. Dust on the sacks of horse, cow, rabbit, goat, dog, cat, and chicken feed. Dust on the salt blocks stacked in the corner, and dust on the hay forks, dung forks, and oats forks hanging on the wall. Dust on the yellow slicker at the ready on a hook next to the door, and dust on the White Owl cigar box full of nuts and bolts.

"Where's the old cat?" I asked, remembering the skinny tortoise-shell perennially nursing a litter of kittens.

"Died about a year ago," Mike said. "We tried keepin' one of the kittens that looked like her, but it got killed out here on the road."

Inside, we paid our bill amid an array of Bag Balm, rat bait, calf nursers, bird feeders, leather gloves, wormers, barn boots, fly swatters, flea collars, heat lamps, and Devil Dust for horses.

A chalkboard listing the daily price for each kind of feed still hung on the back wall, and brooms, chains, shovels, rakes, axes and ax handles were still stationed near the kerosene stove by the back door. Pliers were on special at $4.50 a pair. And a little girl was checking out a pair of leather mittens. Like I said, not much has changed.

The 1980s federal dairy herd buyout worked only for a while. A new initiative is once again being considered to reduce milk supplies and increase prices by taking whole herds out of production. Long ago, the mill belonged to her forebearers, Charlie's wife told me. The building that housed it now is occupied by a pizza parlor, and only one of the three or more feed stores that originally served York Springs remains in business.

Idaville Post Office
April 1995

If you walk into the Idaville Post Office any weekday after school, you'll meet postmaster Mary Grimes and about a half dozen or so of the northern Adams County crossroads community's 32 children. Mary knows exactly how many there are because that's how many presents she put under the post office Christmas tree last year.

"Kids Care!" is the name of a new series of commemorative stamps designed by children that went on sale at Idaville and other U.S. Post Offices yesterday. Last summer, Mary's kids drew pictures for the 1994 national contest that were among the 150,000 entries depicting ways to preserve, protect or restore our environment.

This summer, they'll draw pictures again because Mary cares.

Inside the exemplary Federalist-style, three-brick-thick building is a simple counter with a postal scale, flanked by 110 small combination-lock post office boxes and a turn-of-the-century oak post office front with a small window and a mail slot in which people still prefer to deposit their outgoing mail. On the counter front two signs are posted—one prohibiting loitering, the other stating "No dogs allowed."

Within a few minutes, the room is filled with children: eight-year-old Lacey; 10-year-old twins, Julie and Jamie; 16-year-old Scott, Lacey's big brother; 12-year-old Bobbie; and 14-year-old Mandi, who babysits the twins. Their parents all are box holders here, and they have come to pick up the mail.

Lacey, a blue-eyed blonde with a Kool-Aid mustache, carries a tan rabbit named Butterscotch.

"Lacey is my librarian," Mary tells me, motioning to the shelf of books just under the FBI and postal inspectors' wanted posters.

Lacey tells me that last year she was too young to participate in the stamp contest, but this year she will draw a picture for it. She wears a headband that she pulls up and down over her eyes while commenting that her favorite book is *Green Eggs and Ham*. Lacey's mom comes in and says that sometimes Lacey waits for the school bus in the post office with Mrs. Grimes when she has to leave early for work. Sometimes, Lacey chimes in, she comes over just to show Mrs. Grimes what she's wearing while her mother stands on the porch to see her safely across the road.

The older kids are checking out the wanted posters. Lacey's bunny is hopping along on one of the deep old windowsills where Mary has five flats of seedlings growing. "I just can't see seeds go to waste," Mary offers in explanation.

No, it's not your typical post office. In the big front windows so friendly to plants, children and bunnies, Mary hangs decorations of the season. At Christmas, you'll see crocheted snowflakes in the windows; right now wreaths decorated in summery flowers hang there along with red, white and blue bunting. On the walls hang stuffed, mounted deer heads.

Mary smiles up at an antlered trophy. "Mr. Delp's father shot this the year his son was born." Ask anyone in

29

Idaville, and they'll tell you the Delp family has owned this building forever. On the far side of the room is Mary's collection of antique scales including one very old post office scale with a spring mechanism, and a 1968 airmail scale with a balance beam weight. First-class letters cost six cents to mail in 1968, Mary notes; airmail went for 10 cents. Near the window is a listing and photos of former Idaville postmasters, including two generations of Delps.

"How old are these pictures?" Scott asks about the "wanted" posters. Mary explains that, although the pictures may be old, the file is frequently updated. "That means, if you see a friend of yours in there, you'll still have to report him," she laughs.

A few of the kids pick a piece of candy out of the basket on the counter while the twins' mom comes in, relieved to find them here. Not long ago, there was an accident at the crossroads, and Lacey's mother mentions she may circulate a petition to put a flashing light at the intersection.

"Talk to Pastor Small," Mary offers, "he's got some ideas."

There is talk about summer plans. Mandi would like to work for Mary on the 200-acre farm in the southern end of the county where she and her husband raise cattle and Christmas trees. Mary orders plants—red salvia and white petunias—from Mandi, who is selling them as part of a fundraiser for the United Brethren church just up the road.

Close to 4:30, Mary's kids have cleared out, and my eyes wander back to the "No Loitering and No Dogs Allowed" signs posted at the front of the counter.

"It's your job to be part of the community," Mary says, handing me a half-dozen tomato plants, pepper plants and two sprouts of parsley. "So you're always looking for ways to contribute."

She sees me glancing back at the counter and smiles: "The sign didn't say anything about rabbits, did it?"

Mary Grimes retired, and the Idaville Post Office closed in 2008.

Seek-No-Further for the Perfect Fruit
October 2002

"Seek-No-Further," my friend Teeta Daniels purred when I complimented her on the apple dessert she served along with a story about the main ingredient. Her Seek-No-Further apple tree is an antique variety, she revealed, from Boyer Nurseries and Orchards near Arendtsville. While I suspect my friend, enamored with words, fell for this tree because of its name, her recipe worked beautifully with these apples, which have a sweet firmness and unique personality.

"We don't spray," vouched Teeta's husband, Bill, verifying that the tree produces well, sans pesticides. This is an exceptional quality in orchard country, where every insect within a 10-mile radius is known to zero in on unsprayed fruit.

Boyer Nurseries propagates many antique apples. On a sunny October morning just after a frost, Betty Chronister, who has worked there for 26 years, took me on a tour. Our first stop was the Boyers' St. Martin Farm just off the Mummasburg Road. Despite our recent drought, the Lady apples are a nice size this year. "We've already got orders for these," Chronister said, handing me several of the dainty little bright red and green variety, thought to date back to the fourth century B.C. We drove past a row of crimson Rome apples to the acreage where most of the nursery's antique varieties grow.

Chronister credits Dr. Thomas Lloyd of Mount Gretna with their decision to propagate the antiques. Lloyd, now a professor of health evaluation sciences at the Pennsylvania State University's Milton S. Hershey Medical Center in Hershey, started The Preservation Apple Tree Co. some years back and gave Boyer Nurseries buds to graft on their root stock. Now Boyer sells 150-200 trees of each antique variety annually.

Chronister ticked off the names of these modern incarnations of the centuries-old fruit trees: Freedom, Liberty, Seek-No-Further, Pink Pearl, Black Gilliflower, Sheepnose, Washington Strawberry, Sops of Wine, Gravenstein, Cox's Orange Pippin, and Spitzenberg, her favorite. Each has an enchanting history and a unique appearance.

"Americans gradually forgot what a really good, fresh apple tastes like, just as they prefer fake maple syrup to real," says Roger Yepsen in the beautiful little book, *Apples*, which he wrote and illustrated. In pre-refrigeration America, Yepsen notes, apples were available 11 months of the year, cider was the most popular drink, and pies and tarts were served as bread. His descriptions of these old varieties read like a wine connoisseur's "hints of apricot" reviews, but I will attempt my own from the apples that bulged my pockets after my autumn visit to Boyers.

Fameuse (French for famous) Snow indeed offers a snow-white flesh, somewhat soft but tangy, melt-in-your-mouth sweet—like snow custard—taste. It reminds me of the apples I used to pick on my aunt's farm in Clarion County.

Esopus Spitzenberg, noted by Yepsen to have been Thomas Jefferson's favorite, is a medium size, crisper-than-crisp apple with a pleasing bite. Just the thing you want in your lunch bag.

Lady, which I have also recently bought at the Peters Orchards near my home, is sweet, sweet, sweet and makes a lovely adornment on fresh fir decorations at Christmas time.

Seek-No-Further—my friend's favorite that started this whole, mouth-watering "pippin" of a column—while not the prettiest globe in the orchard, produces a large, firm fruit that smells like your best hayride and barn dance memories. It is so sweet and juicy you expect to be splashed on your second bite. Good for eating and cooking, it makes a wonderful pie.

> *As proof that new crosses can compete with the old varieties, John Aires, a member of the Peters Orchards clan, offers the Honey Crisp, an early apple so sweet and crunchy it tastes like honeysuckle nectar and also makes a lovely pie. In 2009 Adams County ranks 11th nationwide in apple production according to a Pennsylvania Agricultural Extension website.*

Twirly Top
June 1999

The cultural and social hub of Gardners, Pennsylvania—that's Twirly Top. I remember when the daughter of one of my friends came home from school indignant that her teacher had made fun of the popular gathering place. In a more-than-patronizing tone, the man observed to his students that it was a big night in our little crossroads village when "Pa loaded all the kids in the back of his pickup truck and took 'em down to Twirly Top."

Twenty years ago, the girl worked at the drive-in restaurant when she wasn't life-guarding at the state park just down the road. Now her nephew, a high school senior who will head off to college in another year, works at Twirly Top, too. It's a tradition in their family, and a tradition with the Sedells, who have owned and operated the ice cream stand for twenty-five years.

The opening of Twirly Top every year marks the beginning of summer in our out-of-the-way neighborhood.

Alice, matriarch of the Sedell family, says she might as well count on cleaning tables with just one hand every morning because she's constantly returning waves to customers with her other hand. Alice's daughter, Linda, was just sixteen when the family moved here and she got a job at Twirly Top, then owned by the Taylors, next door. When the restaurant came up for sale, the Sedells bought it and the whole family joined Linda, working at Twirly Top.

Linda and her brother worked here until they graduated high school. "I raised two good kids," Alice says. "They had to work. It kept them out of trouble." All the Sedells have other jobs. Linda now works for the phone company.

Alice peels big white onions while we sit at a geranium-adorned picnic table outside the restaurant and talk. "I do all the prep work," she tells me. "We don't have anything low-fat except frozen yogurt. Full of calories and full of taste."

Favorites such as cheeseburger subs and Italian steak subs are all made "fresh as you order," Alice says. She explains that the onions are used on these particular sandwiches, bringing saliva to my mouth with her description of "wafer steaks with melted cheese and fried onions."

"We use only canola oil. Our hamburgers are 100 percent beef—quarter pounders.

"In the summer, we only use home-grown tomatoes. We always have a garden."

Alice is picking strawberries at a local farm these days to make the topping for fresh strawberry sundaes. "You won't get strawberries that taste like jelly," she purrs. Later it will be fresh peach sundaes and peach milkshakes. The same goes for blueberries and black raspberries. All drip over mounds of soft-serve or regular ice cream. "I make my own home-made peanut butter topping," she adds. "My whipped cream is even real whipped cream."

Weekly specials are a big hit with the regulars, who

often request such things as the homemade barbecue.

I offer to Alice that, for my part, one of the best Twirly Top treats is the root beer float featuring vanilla soft-serve that comes in a 16-ounce glass with a whole can of root beer on the side. If Twirly Top just filled the glass like everyone else, you'd get little more than foam. "And that's not fair," according to Alice.

The Sedells are pet lovers, and their menu board includes a "Doggy Treat" dish of vanilla ice cream with two small Milk Bone biscuits on it. Out back, near the flower garden, they also offer a pet station with fresh water for dogs and cats that come by with their owners. On the big bulletin board that faces Route 34, notices appear for PAWS, a local animal welfare organization.

"We have so many repeat customers," Alice brags. "When they walk up to the window, they don't even have to tell us...we know what they want. We'll say, 'Oh here comes the hot dog and the chocolate cone.'" A local doctor with a large family has even bought—"dedicated," Alice says—his own picnic table here.

When she tells me, "We're the Chamber of Commerce, too," I do a double take. "Where's Laurel Lake?" or "Where's the canning factory?" passers-by want to know, and Alice gives directions.

Now Linda will be the new owner, her mother explains. Her fiancé, Chris Thorp, works the afternoon shift every day and manages the restaurant. Chris is a Harvard graduate with a degree in fine arts. He decided to come to Gardners because this is where he wants to spend his life. How's that for culture?

Several years after I wrote this piece, the Washington Post *featured Twirly Top as a road trip from the D.C. area. We gave the article to the Sedells, and they posted it on their bulletin board right next to the picnic tables. Since then, Twirly Top has been sold once and is up for sale again. The popular local hangout sits north of Gardners village, just across the Cumberland County line at the intersection of PA route 34 and Pine Grove Road.*

Chapter 2
An Outlander's Coming of Age
CR

While it often takes an outsider's eye for a fresh perspective on certain subjects, especially in areas steeped in tradition, I learned the hard way that my neighbors had inherited skills and knowledge that are not acquired inside a university. Here, it was unwise to assume that any property improvement would be welcomed by your neighbors or to figure you could make said improvements at your convenience. I remember well the fall my husband took his chainsaw to a rotting pear tree. The next day, our boys came in from playing with the neighborhood children and announced we were all going to drown in a lake of fire, "'Cause dad chopped that tree down on Sunday."

Likewise, it was okay to write about my neighbors' apple butter making but not about something as personal as an estate sale. I wrote early on about quilts and collectibles that were auctioned off to strangers, noting that their late owner, who lived without modern conveniences such as an automatic washing machine, had likely saved these pretty things all her life and died without allowing herself the luxury of their use. In due time, I was informed of the family's indignity. It has taken decades, but I've learned not to be judgmental—a good lesson for any geography.

Do It *Yerself*
June 1983

It was a summer when if something jangled in my pocket, I knew it wasn't change, it was nails—roofing nails, concrete mollies, sinkers, eight-penny, 10-penny, 16-penny, and even 40-penny goonies the force of which would flatten the waffles on your sneaker soles when you tried to hammer them. The nails were a kind of guidepost, for we could tell just where we were on our 12 x 24 feet do-it-yourself solar greenhouse-kitchen addition by the type of nails we were using and happened to have in our pockets at any given time.

It wasn't as if we had to look for things to do on our house. When we began construction, I told my husband, John, that our neighbors would be passing the old paint-peeling 19th-century structure saying, "What are they doing now? They can't even fix up the rooms they have."

We had known not long after we moved into the house that the welcoming old kitchen with walk-in fireplace would not suit our needs and couldn't provide an efficient traffic pattern unless we removed windows and changed the entire look of the place—something we did not want to do. At that time, we decided a simple bump-out addition in another part of the house would provide ample space for a conventional kitchen. But as the fuel crunch squeezed in on us, we began to think solar like so many other people.

Although we had never undertaken anything of this size before, John did a little research, drew up plans, started gathering materials, cleared everything away from the south side of the house and stepped off the dimensions. We began excavation for the foundation—the only job we hired out—right before the Fourth of July, and hit our first snag the night the backhoe left.

At about 10 p.m. we discovered that the toilets weren't flushing. Worse, the children, who were red-clay colored from head to toe and fighting tired after a full day of playing King of the Hill on the bulldozed mounds, couldn't get a bath until we cleared an obstruction in the septic line. Out with the pick. Out with the shovels. Out with the plumber's snake. Out with the flashlights to the refrain of "Why do those kids always use up my batteries?"

It was just the beginning of a summer's work that was to teach me the real meaning of the term *togetherness*.

Unlike most, our solar greenhouse would provide living space for more than plants and, instead of sitting on a gravel bed, it would have a basement. It was in this basement that I was to find that togetherness meant working under conditions no self-respecting union member would tolerate. It meant crawling under the old sewer pipes that had to be temporarily suspended by a delicate system of wires and props until the block work was completed. And sometimes it meant cussing and laughing together when the props gave way and one of us got an impromptu unsanitary shower.

As soon as a concrete floor was poured and seasoned, the basement walls began to rise and I learned another new meaning for an old term. *Striking* wasn't a description of how I would look in my new bathing suit but of what I'd be doing to the mortar my husband laid between the concrete blocks.

Temperatures climbed to 97 and 98 degrees as we worked on the concrete floor in bake-your-brains heat, knowing that if we didn't get this first stage done on schedule we'd never have things ready to close in before winter. Weekends were the time to move: we'd get up early to take advantage of the shade and coolness, rest a short while in the afternoon and work until dark, consuming gallons of iced tea and water in between. When friends called for me, our children could honestly say, "Sorry, she can't come to the phone, she's down in the pits." The boys helped, too, mixing mortar, carrying blocks one at a time, and placing drainage stones along the foundation sides.

When at last the final row of blocks went up, John bolted heavy beams to the supports of the existing house, fitted and jostled floor joists into place, and nailed plywood down to make a floor strong enough, as one friend joked, "to drive a tractor on."

Most of our materials were scrounged. The heavy well-seasoned lumber, for example, was quite sound although it was salvaged from an old building and had splinters enough to put a porcupine to shame. The boards were not consistent in dimension, and each piece had to be fitted individually.

The plans changed from time to time as we worked and John, with typical Rube Goldberg inventiveness, conveniently declared that nothing in conventional solar construction was sacred, allowing the 69-degree slope we chose to give our glass panels. This angle would bring in a maximum of the winter sun's slanted rays and just a minimum of the direct overhead summer rays, he told me as we wedged the heavy timbers in line to form a frame that would soon put us up on our new plywood roof with hammers, nails, roofing paper, shingles, aluminum flashing and tar.

Then came the time to install large three-by-eight feet Thermopane windows. Like the lumber, they too had been scrounged, leftover windows salvaged by a friend when a nearby company remodeled. They were well made, extremely heavy and irreplaceable. We knew if we dropped one, old Rube would have to rework our design again.

Carefully, we teetered the windows on the wooden frames, chiseling a bit of wood here and there to achieve the proper fit. We slid them into place, framed them with fascia board, bolted the various layers together and caulked all the seams.

By early November, we had sheathed the addition walls with foam insulation board, added wooden siding, treated all the wood with preservative, and installed a side window, vents and a roof exhaust fan for summer ventilation. Then we insulated the whole thing just in time to get our first "free" heat of the winter season. We picked the last splinters out of our hands and settled back to marvel at the 90-degree temperatures our solar addition gave us to circulate through the house while the outside air hovered in the 20s and 30s.

Now with the arrival of spring, John is getting ready to rip out the walls, opening up the part of the house that adjoins the addition so we can start work on our new kitchen. A skeptic at first, he is pleased with the success of our first real building project. I, too, am impressed. If it weren't for all this fun, next time I think I might just say, "Do it yourself, John."

Our first attempt at solar heat wasn't as successful as we'd hoped. Despite repeated caulking, the angled glass panes of our solar addition always leaked and never really lessened our heating bill much. We eventually replaced the slanted walls with vertical ones, traditional double-hung windows, and a French door that opens to a deck where we sit, spring through fall, and watch the birds.

First Pig
May 1983

George was a pig from the start. The runt of the litter, we got him free from a friend who suggested we'd be doing

41

him a favor to take the puny weanling from his mother, as his siblings were picking on him.

It was up to my husband, John, to pick the pig up on the way home from work, wrap him in a burlap bag and tie the end with twine. Simple, he thought—until a grunting, scuffling noise from the back seat of the old Ford station wagon revealed that George had squeezed halfway out of his sack and was running hog-wild through the family car.

John screeched to the side of U.S. Route 15 amidst rush-hour traffic and, knees on the front seat, arms in the back, wrestled a squealing pink piglet while passing motorists gawked, doubtless looking for the woman being accosted in broad daylight.

George wriggled completely free of the burlap bag. A frustrated John got him halfway back in before he gave up and drove home. I got to clean the car.

No matter, now we had livestock and our newly acquired 21-acre homestead with aging house and barns could claim farm status once again. Truth was, we had a pig—our neighbors had hogs. We bought pig feed and gleaned corn from nearby fields after the fall harvest. George grew fat and happy and developed a cordial relationship with John, who visited with him each evening and informed me of the superior intelligence and character of swine.

Months passed, and we became accustomed to having a pig around, albeit with the knowledge that market day would inevitably arrive. When friends came to visit one Sunday afternoon, John asked their 14-year-old son, a 4-H swine producer, if George would be ready soon. The boy took one look at our pig and laughed, "Well, don't *drive* him to market [old-timers used to 'drive' their livestock on foot to the nearest town]—he'll have a heart attack!"

George was fat, but pigs are supposed to be fat, we

thought. The ideal weight for a hog was 200-250 pounds, and we conceived that to be immense. After all, one couldn't ask a pig to step on the bathroom scale.

We arranged with a local butcher to take our portly pig as soon as possible and waited for his call. The phone rang late one rainy evening just as John lumbered in the driveway after a harrowing return from a business trip to Philadelphia. No time for supper or sentimentality: George had to be there that night. Amid the morass of spring mud, the little livestock trailer eventually was backed up to the pigpen. We dropped the tailgate and scattered straw over the slippery bed. It would be a snap, John said. George would think we'd added a room to the pigpen; he'd walk right in and lie down for a snooze.

George wasn't sleepy. He was annoyed.

The pig eyed our subterfuge, snorted and ran back into his pen, smashing John against the wall along the way. We decided to give him a "last supper" incentive by placing apples up the tailgate to lure him from the pen and into the trailer. George loved apples, we reasoned, and would literally eat his way to market.

He rooted at the apples but tasted only those within snout's reach. For the next three hours John and I wistfully considered the intellect of pigs, as one maneuver after another failed to entice George. We blocked the pen entrance with straw bales, fashioned a rope harness to use on him like a pulley, lassoed him with two harnesses when that didn't work, and tried to joke that this must be how the term *hog-tied* came to be.

George stubbornly sat his 400-pound bulk down.

Mud mingled with manure. We wallowed, we groaned, we pushed, we pulled—and George got mad. When just one last tug was needed to slide him across the tailgate, he screamed and fell with a leaden thud. Just as no manure is as rank as that hauled out of hog pens, no sound inspires terror more than a pig scream. "That's it. He probably broke his leg!" John cried. George wasn't moving. Our pig promised to turn into a prodigious pumpkin until truck lights appeared in a neighbor's driveway. "Call him," my beleaguered husband commanded.

In five minutes the farmer, Paul "June" Bupp, appeared and sized up the situation with an amused glance. "You grab his tail and push when I take a-hold of his ears," he told John. Slick as a pig's whistle, without apples or ropes, George was up on all fours, amazingly recovered, in the trailer and on his way to the butcher.

Still, it seemed destined that our first pig would never become Sunday dinner. A short while after we'd picked up our pork and stacked the neatly wrapped packages of sausage, chops and loin roasts in our freezer, the second-hand appliance broke down and we lost everything in it. Since then, we've learned how to grow grain for our own livestock feed and how to approximate the market weight of animals.

We've raised two hogs nearly every year, but somehow none has ever compared to our first—good old George.

A pig sounded like a good idea. We had a goat, but early on we determined we needed more live-stock if we were going to call ourselves a farm. Wouldn't it be good for the boys to have chores, to take responsibility for something other than their toys? Overrun by honeysuckle, multi-flora rose and nightshade, our place had not supported animals for decades. Work on the house stopped while we cleared the pastures, cut locust trees for fence posts, dug new postholes and strung wire fencing.

We didn't know until it was much too late for George—who, in fact, was not injured in the comedy of errors that ensued as we hauled him off to

*market—that there was a simple way to mark a
pig's growth progress:*

Taking care not to excite the pig, use a string to
measure the distance around its chest and its
length from head to rear. Then, apply the following
formula for approximating livestock weight: Heart
Girth multiplied by Heart Girth, multiplied by
Length, divided by 400. For example, a pig with a
heart girth measuring 50 inches and a length of 52
inches, weighs approximately 325 pounds.

Outlandish Outlanders
June 1983

It was during a vacation to Massachusetts that I first
heard the term *outlander*. The word was used by an elderly native as the ultimate insult in his description of the
people moving into the "wee-ahd" (weird)-looking development down the street. He considered the jutting, mod-
ernistic structures a blight on Amherst, the town where
Emily Dickinson once lived and wrote, and was quick to
blame this and other evils on the shady outlanders.

A few years later I moved to south-central Pennsylvania and was reminded of the term when I telephoned local
fuel suppliers. Winter was coming and we needed heat. I
inquired about the cost of fuel oil and explained that I was
a new resident who wanted to be a customer.

"Well, who are you?" asked the voice on the other end
of the line.

I reiterated my name, address and approximate location.

"NO, I mean just WHO are you?" the voice demanded.

"Uh-oh," I said to myself. "I am an outlander."

After recounting my life history, including my town of
birth, my former address, my reason for moving and my
husband's present place of employment, I got on the list of

privileged—not preferred—customers.

In addition to making introductory apologies for being an immigrant, I soon discovered that when giving directions to my home it was advantageous to refer to it as the old Alton Miller place even though Alton hadn't lived in it for several years and I had optimistically painted "Graham" on the mailbox.

Since then, I've come to accept the outlander assignation with grudging good humor and have even formulated a definition for it: *outlander, noun. 1. Foreigner. 2. A person not having three generations of relatives residing in or near his present home. 3. Anyone with a funny-sounding name. 4. A government employee. 5. A registered Democrat. 6. Anyone not born here.*

Once the definition is understood, it follows that a whole list of universal truths is also revealed:

- Outlanders will move in next to a farm, demand sidewalks and streetlights, and complain about the way things smell.
- Outlanders always want to change things: i.e., they want art and music in the schools.
- Taxes increase in direct proportion to the number of outlanders in the community.
- The offspring of outlanders do not play baseball as well as the children of natives because their feet are genetically unsuited to the local terrain.
- Outlanders often appear at social events in dude clothing.
- Outlanders spoil their wives by giving them automatic clothes washing machines and dryers.
- Outlanders are responsible for a plethora of useless services such as trash collection and water conditioning.
- Communist tendencies lurk behind every outlander's smile.

• Natives are permitted to accept outlanders only after a probationary period, at which time they may be trusted within limits.

After we'd lived here a while, I became acquainted with other outlanders—you know the old sayings about birds of a feather, misery wants company, etc.—and discovered a pecking order within our ranks. "How long have you been here?" a fellow outlander might ask. There are, I learned, 10-year outlanders, five-year outlanders, and neophyte outlanders. The neophytes are characterized by wild-looking eyes and sometimes calm themselves by paging through the phone book, finding other people who are the sole entry under their family name.

In addition, there are outlanders who come from other places within the same county, as in the case of a man I know who moved to my area from an adjacent village more than 30 years ago and still considers himself an outlander because he wasn't born right here.

Unlike the southerner who said he was 16 years old before he knew the term *damned Yankee* was two words, most natives here don't usually come right out and say what they think of outlanders. They stoically accept the fact that aliens have invaded paradise. They seem curious about and sometimes grateful for our eccentricities. And they are always willing to extend a helping hand in time of need. Yet they watch us with a cocked eye, waiting for the chameleon to change colors, silently reminding us that they were here first.

When I put myself in their place, I can appreciate the chagrin of those first American natives, the Indians, as they watched white men get off the boat and propose civilization to them. Surely they thought, "If things were so great where they came from, then why are they here?"

Many a local forebear came here directly from Europe, mostly Germany. Here the average person moves only once in his life, when he is married. Indeed it is that same unspoiled provinciality and Old World faith in the value of hard work and independence that have drawn us outlanders here. When we go back to where we were born, we find that it is simply where we came from and that this now is our home, the only place we ever want to live—Paradise.

And we, too, are on our guard against aliens. In fact, just the other day I heard that two farms in our neighborhood have been sold to developers. Before you know it, they'll be insisting on sidewalks and streetlights. Outlandish!

Despite the fact that my husband and I have lived in it longer than any of its owners except John Guise, who built it in the 1800s, our house continues to be known as the old Alton Miller place.

Raccoon Raconteur
June 1983

Johnny Everhart is Davy Crockett, James Thurber, and Peter Pan all rolled into one wiry little man. This year he was named Skunk Trapper of the Year by District Eight of The Pennsylvania Trappers Association. But Johnny insists that trapping skunks is not what he does best; he's best at trapping raccoons and, on occasion, he even wears a coonskin cap he made himself.

Still, anyone who knows him knows that what Johnny's best at isn't trapping or fishing, hiking, camping or any of the mountain-man pastimes he relishes. What Johnny Everhart truly shines at is storytelling and the manly art of graphic conversation.

At 63, he's a trapper in winter, a fisher in summer, and a raccoon raconteur all year 'round. In a hurry-up world, he's his own man with time to spare for children, neighbors, and local writers or anyone who appreciates a good yarn embellished with a roguish, little-boy sense of humor. Ten years ago, when he had a chance at early retirement from his government job, Johnny went home and thought about it. All it took was one night's sleep filled with dreams of how he'd be his own boss, go out and check his traps early in the morning and come home to fall asleep in front of the wood stove, a free man.

His independence wasn't a newfound thing. John was born in the old York Springs tollhouse, where his mother was the last toll keeper on the Hanover to Carlisle Pike. The brother of four married sisters, he exclaims, "Me? I'm still a bachelor. Never got married. There's too much world freedom out there for me to get hooked up!" On the wall hangs an old family portrait that shows the Everharts and their five children holding the family pets: a white rabbit, several cats and a pigeon. Words literally crack from him as he tells how he's been trapping and camping since he was eight years old. He still cherishes an old camp trophy he whittled with a pocketknife at Pine Grove in the summer of 1938, the year before he graduated high school.

Just a few years ago, he whittled another set of trophies, commemorating his hike along a 10-mile stretch of the Appalachian Trail one cold day in January. "When I got to my sixtieth birthday, I kept tellin' myself that I wanted to hike the Appalachian Trail while I could still do it. And I had three lads [ages 10-15] who wanted to go along." Each one took a hand-whittled trophy home.

Trapping season begins in November. That's when Johnny starts rising at 3 a.m., working his trap line until 10 a.m. or later, depending on the weather. "I don't take anybody along, don't give any demonstrations. I don't give away none of my secrets," he chuckles.

John makes some of his own traps. He makes his own tags, fur boards, and many of his tools. But the thing he takes most pride in is the concocting of his own secret animal lures. And what are those mysterious lures made of? Generally speaking, it's a list of things that ought to be included in a boyhood chant along with "great big gobs of greasy, grimy gopher guts." Specifically, he's not telling. "There's always tricks with trappin'," he chortles. But he will give a show-and-smell demonstration of some of the base ingredients. "Here, smell," he snickers. "That one'll tear you up. That's pure fox gland."

Trapping foxes is what Johnny would most like to be best at. Now he has an award for trapping skunks, and he's well-known for the number and quality of raccoon pelts he brings in—62 in a good year—but the fox often eludes him. "When you're trappin' fox, you'll try anything," he says, opening a treasure chest of crusty amber-colored bottles and tiny plastic squeeze flasks. On the yellowed labels are names that would bring tears to the eyes of the witches in *Macbeth*: beaver caster, 100-percent pure skunk essence, muskrat musk, fox urine, Russian anise oil, mink musk, oil of lovage, ambrette tincture, and others. They assail the nose with their sweet, yeasty, tainted odors. Alongside them is a collection of old pop bottles, coffee jars and a few whiskey bottles filled with the moldering colors of green, yellow, mud brown, cocoa brown and amber-colored meat—marinating, Johnny says—waiting to become part of his secret recipes.

Many of his lures are food-or gland-based and include musk or urine and a preservative. Musk, he notes, is the base for many fine perfumes. There are also "call lures" for attracting animals from a distance. When he mixes his recipes, he uses rubber gloves or a pair of old canvas gloves that have been soaked in fox urine. "The fox definitely survives on his snout," he says, warning that any hint of human scent will scare the animal away. To get rid of it, the traps are boiled in a black oil-based compound, then waxed with paraffin and beeswax.

"You don't lay nothin' down," when setting a trap, Johnny cautions, demonstrating how he carries his tools in a converted apple-picking bag and takes as few steps as possible when approaching a site. He uses three sets: dirt hole, urine post, and flat set. He works quickly, sifting dirt over the hole set, for example, and backs out of the site. Traps must be kept immaculate, as the fox will not come to the smell of rust.

Pelts and meat are stored in an extra freezer. "We eat the meat," he says, describing the gastronomical delight of barbecued raccoon cooked in a steel frying pan over an open fire. "All wild meat should be cooked with an open lid," he advises.

His trap line covers an eight-mile stretch by vehicle, with additional walk-in distance, and includes the land of many grateful farmers. "He really saved our pond," said one, recounting the damage done by muskrats. Johnny spends his off-hours whittling wooden gifts he calls *tokens* for the farmers.

"I never killed another animal I found caught in my traps," he claims, reciting a litany of lost and undernourished dogs and cats he's nursed back to health.

At winter's end, he dons his coonskin cap and packs his pelts off to the district rendezvous, where trappers from this part of the state meet to sell their furs. One year he took a record 346 muskrat pelts. For those who disapprove, he cautions that trapping is merely a way of weeding out the weak and unfit. "You know, they're afraid of the skunks and raccoons spreadin' rabies." However, the encroachment of suburbia into Adams County is having its effect, he says: "You can make a fox set [on farmland] this year, and next year they're diggin' a [septic system]

51

perk hole.

"But I'm not much of a sitter," Johnny muses, adding that next year he'll try for the skunk trophy again. His gaze moves to the back of the barn where several home-made kites of different sizes and colors hang. "You know, the biggest majority of people that don't have a lot of fun in life give up. They just don't try," he laughs.

At age 88, Johnny Everhart gave up running a trap line on the advice of his doctor. He remains vigorous, still lives on his own and has set up the living room of his old farmhouse as a kind of museum for his various trophies. Though he has a girlfriend, Johnny has never married.

Corn Planter Catharsis
June 1983

I am mourning the passing of a tradition far more significant to me than any national holiday and of greater value than the costliest Christmas gift. Unlike on traditional holidays with their stressful buildup and near-certain letdown, on Corn Planting Day, I always knew what to expect. I put a lot into it but I got something back that lasted all year. It required a year's planning and hoarding and a tremendous expenditure of energy, and it was worth it.

Never fail, rain or shine, I was rewarded by the annual tradition of our one great, good colossal fight of the year. I could count on it. It happened every year on the day set aside for sowing our several acres of field corn, and all winter long I saved up my wifely woes for the spring corn planter catharsis.

Like many old customs, it has fallen by the wayside of the road to modern life and is as sadly obsolete as the old corn planter, now laid to rest in a shed at the edge of our property. The rust-pocked, two-row John Deere was held together with wire and duct tape and had a draw bar that could be attached to a horse or mule or our vintage model Farmall-H. Its two small seed canisters relied on drop plates so old that local feed dealers scratched their heads in amazement and had to dig in the back of their mill storage to find a variety of corn that would sift down through. Those seeds always had names such as "Cornell" that were themselves an American history lesson.

While everyone else planted eight rows of modern hybrid marvels at a time, we limped along with historic seeds, a roll of duct tape, and a bucket of fertilizer. Directly behind the seed canisters rode two fertilizer bins and the lacy iron seat—leaning to one side if you looked at it with your head held straight—on which I perched. It was my job to bump on behind in that catbird seat and ascertain that the vintage gears and pulleys were clinking along as expected, delivering their payload to furrows that the John Deere's metal tines scored in our rough ground. Hydraulics hadn't been thought of when our machine was marketed. So, at the end of every row, I had to push an iron lever that put the whole gizmo in limbo until the corner was turned and yell "okay" to my husband, John, driving the tractor, when all was ready to start planting the next row. The flaking iron lever worked reluctantly and always took a few layers of hand along with it. Disregarding the fact that my feet had to wedge somewhere between the moving chain pulleys, the whole thing was a relatively simple operation—when it worked.

In reality, it would have been easier to plant the two acres by hand: three fishes to a hole, a rain dance, etc. But that never would have yielded the purgative powers of the corn planter catharsis.

I could count on the planter breaking down at about the middle of the second row. Fixing it required only a yell of "whoa," with John jumping down from the tractor to wiggle a widget or two and get the mechanism back on track. Then a complacence settled over the whole humming, clinking scene, lulling me into daydreams focused on the sky or the dogwood blossoms in the adjacent woods. My thoughts invariably drifted far from the dry dirt and little pellets of fertilizer and seed, only to be rudely awakened by exhortations spilling out of the dust between me and the tractor:

"Didn't you hear that damned thing clunking? Now we have to go back and double-plant this whole &%$#-ing row and we'll never beat the rain. You don't pay attention to anything I say!"

Grimy-faced, cramped legs wrapped around my ears or caught in the malfunctioning pulleys, I aroused from reverie. "Yes, I do! It's not my fault the dumb thing doesn't work—it's falling apart. Besides, I never signed up to be a farmer's wife anyhow."

"Well, nobody asked you to!"

"That's not true! I always spend time helping you, and just when do you spend any time working on the house? I'm gonna be 90 years old before that kitchen is ever finished. By then I won't remember how to cook anything!"

"You don't remember anything anyway..."

"Well, these darned fertilizer bins aren't helping. There's no lids on 'em. I'll bet I'm getting nitrogen poisoning from all the fertilizer dust I've inhaled."

"It's all your imagination!"

I used that same imagination to deduce that the missing bin lids were probably lost sometime back in the 1940s when another corn planter jockey threw them at her tractor driver during a similar fray.

It was an elaboration of all our male-female disagreements: he was in the driver's seat, while I was eating his dust; I wasn't paying attention when he needed me. It was purely and wonderfully verbal. It was the best, most flamboyant fight of the whole year, a spring purge better than all the old-time tonics and a lot more fun than sulfur and molasses. We savored it, knowing there would be no hard feelings later and that the planting never failed to get done because it absolutely required the two of us, just as everything else in our life. We were far enough away from the kids not to be heard, and the machinery made such a racket that the neighbors took in nothing worse than a scene punctuated by waving arms and bobbing heads. When it was done, the air would be as clear and fresh as after a spring rain.

Then one day last year, the old planter was retired by a riderless four-row model, and I wondered if our marriage would survive the loss of the spring tradition. I needn't have worried, though. That very night we discussed the prospects of acquiring a vintage model hay baler.

Eventually, we gave the old two-row John Deere corn planter to a neighbor who collects antique farming equipment.

Cheep Cheep
November 1983

Now that the statute of limitations has expired, I am free to confess my crime. It all started one cloudless June day more than three years ago. My husband, John, was mowing hay at the scene of the crime, a ripe timothy patch, when the victim came strutting out onto an adjacent road. In a matter of minutes, he walked straight into our clutches.

"Mom, come look. It's a baby pheasant!" our sons yelled. "Can we keep it, can we?" Over my protests—I had always suffered a phobia of birds that made me itch every time I got within 100 feet of a hen house—the tiny chick was ensconced in an empty shoebox by the time John came in from his farm work.

"Must've disturbed the nest," he said. "The mother won't take him back now. Doesn't look like he's more'n a couple a days old."

"Please, Mom, we gotta keep him. He'll die if we don't feed him." They knew right where to get me, though I was well aware that our state's game laws proscribe harboring a wild pheasant.

What does one feed a pheasant chick? A phone call to a friend with a flock of barred rock hens gave us a fowl watering dish and a supply of finely ground corn. Now we were hopelessly involved. We mixed the chicken scratch with water, and the boys fed him with an eyedropper. When he seemed to be failing, we called an elderly neighbor, who advised getting him out of doors, closer to his natural habitat. The next day, the neighbor dropped by to inspect John's hastily constructed chicken wire pen. The chick was improving. After a while, the old man put his hand to his chin and said, "Don'tcha know it's against the law to keep a pheasant?"

I looked at the pen and knew we were nailed. Was I a perpetrator or an accomplice? "Oh well, we'll just have to hope nobody squeals on us," I mumbled, changing the topic of conversation to pole beans. Now we had implicated an innocent bystander.

Cheep-Cheep, as he was christened, due to the onomatopoetic nature of his chirping, pecked in the grass and gained in strength with each passing day. At night he came back in the house to his Kinney's shoebox bed while I tried to keep an eye out in case old Spook, our cat, ventured into the house. In a few days, he graduated to a grocery store cardboard box.

Cheep was a gregarious chap and seemed fond of

human company, especially that of our elder son. Kirk held and cuddled the chick in total disregard for his allergies to anything with fuzz or hair. The bird scampered up his chest to snuggle in the blonde wisps at the nape of the 11-year-old's neck, murmuring soft chirps while the hair on my neck stood on end. Our chicken-keeping friend did some research and told us that pheasant chicks have a body temperature of 107 degrees and, therefore, naturally seek such warm-body contact. They also are not infested with chicken lice, she assured me—after I'd dusted the little bird with flea powder.

In a short time, Cheep-Cheep seemed less of a wild creature, and my phobia faded. He wasn't a bird. He was a handful of yellow and brown striped fluff on toothpick legs, and he nestled his way into all of our hearts. We watched as, day by day, the fluff became feathers and he spread his newfound wings. He seemed to be going through a kind of puberty, developing a long, gawking pheasant neck and stretching his skinny bird legs behind him, flamingo-style.

The whole family participated in a Saturday morning ritual of swatting houseflies for Cheep-Cheep's breakfast. Those flies could have been bacon and eggs, the way he came running, clipping along behind us, until a fateful morning when his feet weren't swift enough and one Lilliputian leg crunched under the weight of a work shoe. "Oh no, Cheep," John sighed. My husband held the fragile leg while I made a splint, reconsidering the now-obvious wisdom of the game laws and wondering how we could ever return a handicapped bird to its natural environment.

The time came for a family reunion in Pittsburgh, and a friend agreed to pheasant-sit the hobbling bird for us. We returned to a miracle: Cheep-Cheep was walking unimpaired again, and those long, neck-gawking, leg-stretching promenades were back.

Soon it was impossible to keep him in his cardboard house, which by this time was an industrial-size toilet paper box. One morning I went upstairs to find him roosted in Kirk's bed. Another time, he appeared perched in the driver's seat of a Legos car. One night after supper, he did a lift-off from the tall cardboard box and flew into my dishpan of hot water—I'd wanted a birdbath out under the maple trees, but this was bizarre. The chick seemed to have developed a taste for music and frequently made three-point landings on the harp of the piano. Pheasants are reputed to fly only when frightened, but within a few months Cheep was happily learning to become an expert navigator...and bombardier. In my time, I had cleaned up toad "stools" in the cellar and woolly bear caterpillar beads in empty coffee cans, but whitewash on the ivories was too much. It was time for this wild thing to go home.

After several half-hearted attempts with the familiar pheasant neck bobbling along behind me, up and down, in and out, following me home puppy-dog style, Cheep-Cheep eventually returned to stay in the woods near his hay field. I knew it was the right thing to do, but my heart broke.

When small game season opened that fall for the shooting of male pheasants, commonly known as ring-necks or cockbirds, I felt like the witch in Hansel and Gretel—especially after several neighbors reported seeing a tame pheasant. Kirk flew in the kitchen one afternoon, shouting that he'd seen the bird.

"It was Cheep for sure. And, guess what, mom?" he cried in relief, "He's a hen!"

Wild ring-necked pheasants have become a rarity in our neighborhood.

Election Day at Huntington Nos. 1 and 2
May 1984

A worn American flag hung vertically behind the neatly lettered sign fashioned a few years back by Bob Griffith. And a barnyard full of Bill Wenger's steers munched and watched as 106 voters trickled into Huntington Township's No. 2 polling place, a cement block garage wedged into a curve along the Idaville Road. It was the fourth primary election to be held at Wenger's farm.

Jessie Koontz, minority inspector, was there just as she had been for the past 27 years when voting had been done in Bob and Rosie Griffith's garage. And in Yeagy's garage before that. And in the old Idaville schoolhouse long before that.

The schoolhouse is gone now. "Different people have came and went," said Jessie, and the voting has picked up a little over the years. And Huntington Township still has two polling places for its sprawling rural community.

But there's been some talk that county commissioners are considering consolidating the polls, combining the 205 registered voters of Huntington No. 2 with the 488 of Huntington No. 1. Bill Wenger, who built his garage with a room in back just to accommodate elections, said he's not in favor of centralization in this case: "Maybe it's just nostalgic, but I wouldn't want to lose something of value."

Wenger and George Peters, judge of elections at No. 2, complained about the tiny Fourth of July giveaway-size flag the commissioners had provided them as they hung their own borrowed banner Tuesday morning and talked about the effects of county decisions on local people. It was 7:30 a.m. and four residents had voted. "Rural people are so used to accommodating the real changes that artificial changes don't have any reality for them," Peters remarked. He sat at the head of a table in the room in back and announced the voters as they approached the garage. Formal procedure indicates that voters should show their registration cards to match with the information on file, but here nearly every face is familiar and needs no verification.

"Are you better, Catherine?" majority inspector Joyce King inquired as two elderly ladies picked up the paper ballots they would deposit later in the big tin ballot box. The women are neighbors, both widows. Many of the smaller precinct's voters are older and might not travel the added distance if a consolidation were to occur, King noted.

A husband and wife entered a little later: one, a registered Republican, the other a Democrat. And soon another voter arrived on a bicycle, removing her helmet and gloves before coming in to pick up her ballot.

"It's a beautiful day out there," smiled one gentleman as he signed the obligatory certification card with a work-worn hand.

"I always read what I sign," said another and went on to mark his ballot to the melody of the theme from the motion picture *ET*, which he whistled over the canvas sides of one of three Huntington No. 2 voting booths.

Over coffee and donuts during the slack times, there was talk of how Harry Hoffman acquired the goat that grazes with his cows in a neighboring meadow and of what might happen if the county went to voting machines.

Things were pretty much the same at Huntington's No. 1 polling place, now located on Trolley Road in the township municipal building, where people came and went all day and a total of 273 ballots had been counted by a little past midnight.

A young mother was offered baby-holding service, while a local resident provided his own story-telling service when someone inquired about an ambulance that had been sighted near his place that morning. Needlework was taken up, a jangling telephone answered and a potluck lunch eaten by the election workers during the afternoon, while barrel-chested farmers filtered in and out along with seamstresses on lunch break from a nearby dress factory. Everyone recognized state workers who appeared in their day-off clothes during working hours.

Mabel Grove, Huntington No. 1 majority inspector, knew the name of nearly every face that came in the door; and pleasantries were exchanged as voters waited their turns or asked what to do with the tear-off number on the corner of the ballot.

"How's your mother, Ray?" someone inquired of one voter, as they all heard the details of another's recent surgery. Tales were recounted about the year the lights went out in the old election house and they tallied the votes by candlelight. And it was hoped that this year there wouldn't be too many Mickey Mouses or Donald Ducks written in on the ballots, as every write-in has to be recorded and there were years when they'd been counting until 1 or 2 a.m. The conversation touched on politics, skirted religion, and settled on voting machines and the talk of consolidation.

Yes, something would be lost here, too, if consolidation becomes a reality. It would be sleep, unless the county turns to voting machines.

But no one seemed much worried about losing his job. At a rate of $40 or $45, depending on the number of voters, for as much as 19 hours' work, some could think of better things to do.

Still, they joked about the oath they must swear that they will not "vexatiously" delay or refuse to permit any person to vote and that they are not directly or indirectly interested in any bet or wager on the result of the election. Then they discussed their potluck menu for the next election day, in November.

*Huntington 1 and 2 did consolidate into one polling
place in the Huntington Township municipal building. As of 2009, Adams County had not adopted voting machines and still used paper ballots.*

Stolen R.D.
November 1984

Help! I'm the victim of a crime. Someone has stolen
my R.D.

When I was a kid we moved to the country. Ever since
then I've received my mail via Rural Free Delivery and
automatically attached an R.D. number to my identity
along with millions of Americans who have been getting
mail this way since 1896.

It was part of the American tradition. It was the way
I lived and, wherever I moved, I managed to have an R.D.
number.

I was rural, I was free and I was pleasantly anony-
mous. When someone strange asked where I lived, I could
get off the hook with a simple R.D. 1 or R.D. 2, putting a
lot of territory between me and the outside world. I didn't
have street lights or sidewalks or "curb your dog" signs. I
didn't have fights with neighbors; in fact, many times
there were no neighbors.

I was not like ticky tacky—just another number in a
city or suburban development—I was Rural Free Delivery.

Now, in the name of progress, my R.D. has been taken
away. With the stroke of a typewriter key, my county officials have robbed me of a lifelong identity and left me
with a street number and another name to spell. I feel as
if Santa took my chimney and left me a pile of cinders.

While they are telling me that this new house-num-
bering system will help ambulance, fire and police serv-

ices to find me in times of crisis, I am wondering what it portends for the future.

Does this mean my mailman is going to start wearing Bermuda shorts and aviator sunglasses? Does it mean I should quit leaving him cookies?

They have advised me that I should post this new number on both sides of my mailbox in letters at least one inch high and of contrasting color with the box. I wonder what colors contrast with rust and how I'm going to write on a box that is blanketed with privet hedge and poison ivy.

I wonder if this means officials are going to update the little flag on the side of the box that was an important signal in the days before junk mail when the mailman didn't have to stop every day. Maybe we'll be required to supplant the flag with flashing lights. We might use red for times when we want the ambulance or the state police (my municipality doesn't have its own police force) or blue for fire trucks, similar to the bubble gum lights our volunteer firemen affect atop their Broncos.

Perhaps in their zeal for progress they'll even supply us with homing devices and little beepers: "Hey, Pa. What's got those cows in such a ruckus?" "Nothin', Ma. It's just that darned house-findin' beeper."

To implement the new house numbering system, I'm told the people in charge of emergency services will be given grid maps plotting the location of each and every residence and eliminating all probability of error when they try to figure out why my house is number nine when I am less than 20 feet from the start of the road or why my neighbor five doors down is number 281. The issuing of these maps is a tremendous stroke of optimism in an area where not long ago municipal records were stored in Harry's basement or Bertha's attic and at the mercy of mice or squirrels. It wasn't too many years back that supervisors of my own township couldn't remember who had the information about exactly where the township line lay.

This new policy couldn't have come at a worse time for me. Just a few months ago I bought 5,000 business cards, all beautifully engraved with my name and R.D. They were cheaper in quantity and I figured they'd last me for a while.

Now I have to inform my bank, my boss, my garbage man, my insurance company, magazine publishers and many others about my new address. And I have to tell my faraway friends about the change without making them feel obligated for a housewarming gift. The federal government will supply me with handy little postcards to notify everybody and will even pay the postage if I mail within 90 days. I guess this timing could be an advantage if I filled out the information in red and green ink and sent the cards as this year's Christmas greetings.

Still, I am suspicious of things such as this that erase monumental aspects of history in the name of progress. Next thing you know, they'll tell me I have to tear down the outhouse that came with our farm. Then, where will I put all their progress?

Our outhouse still stands adjacent to the barn but its shake shingle roof is in bad repair and the walls list to one side. A passerby stopped one day and offered to buy it—we declined.

Fledgling
September 1985

I thought we'd never make it to his sixteenth birthday. He thought so, too. It seemed interminable, that distance between fifteen and a half and sixteen.

"It's a miracle I lived this long," he gasped with typical teenage dramatics. I look at him now in the driver's seat of the family station wagon and I think, "He's still just a fledgling." But, unlike baby birds that sometimes must be coaxed to leave the nest, he is eager to spread his wings.

"Awe, c'mon, Mom," he pleads, wondering why I'm dragging my feet, never guessing that as he sheds his cocoon, I am spinning mine, protection for a future empty nest. He is in such a hurry. For him there is no past or future. There is no yesterday or tomorrow. There is only now, right now. The anxious, breathless *now*.

How could I expect him to remember the sweet black nights I rocked him to the rhythm of the katydids? His first words? His first steps? His first fever? Only time will cure the fever he has now.

"Whoa, whooaa!" I say. "Don't you think you overshot that intersection just a bit?"

"Well, maybe just a little," he laughs, his voice cracking with adolescent embarrassment.

"Oops," he mutters. The brakes grab, I grab for an armrest and squeeze my eyes into a protective fist against the fast-approaching tailgate just beyond the windshield. It's our first day to test the driver's permit. We try stoplights, left turns and parking lots. He uses the skills his father has taught him in our field to navigate the busy traffic circles of several neighboring small towns. We stop for lunch and he carries the car keys. He takes care of the check—with my money. One minute he's Superman, the next he's still a fledgling.

He talks dreamily of his first car, an old Chevy Nova now sitting in the driveway with primer on its pieces. He buys shiny silvered parts for its engine and a macho muffler to replace the lifetime Muzzler that makes it sound too much like a family vehicle. For his birthday, there is a fancy radio that will never know Beethoven. Later, he will hook it up to speakers that should be accompanied by mandatory earplugs.

Often he sits in my kitchen, legs apart, elbows on his knees, discussing horsepower with his father.

"Stop!" I want to say. "Wait!" I want to warn. "Don't grow up so soon..." I want to cry. But I settle for a lecture on fast cars and fast times, thankful that the Chevy's horsepower, like the mare in our pasture, has mellowed with maturity.

"I found a good book for you at the library," I mention. But *Billy Budd* doesn't stand a chance next to *Road and Track*, *Motorweek*, or the *Auto Locator*.

A friend laments her difficulty with a sixteen-year-old daughter, and I casually discourse on the need to trust.

"Mom, why don't you *ever* trust me?" he moans. How can I expect him to know that it's not he, our firstborn, that I doubt—but myself, the job I've done parenting? One minute he's a volcano, the next he is a puppy. "When I start dating," he ventures, skipping along to another point in the conversation while my heart stops and we drive into town for another lesson in parallel parking.

The road is a straightaway here, tree-lined and warmed by the colors of late summer. My mind drifts, and I remember a story about eaglets I saw not long ago on television. At the beginning, the birds are fledglings, wobbling out of their nest for the first time; in the end, baby fluff gone, they wear the pale black feathers of juveniles—flying, gliding, soaring.

I look at him in the driver's seat, peach fuzz growing into manhood, and I want to cry and smile at once.

"You're doing great," I tell him, proudly. "You're a good driver. I'm relaxed with you driving. Really, I am."

"Yeah, mom—all but your right foot," he says, smiling and nodding toward the floorboard. I self-consciously laugh, crossing my brake foot over my left leg and thinking, "It's a miracle I've lived this long."

*Every six months or so, we measured our boys
against the yellow-enameled doorjamb in our old
kitchen. Kirk seemed to progress upward by mere
fractions of inches. But the year he learned to drive,
he blossomed. With money saved from odd jobs, he
bought his first car and paid for his own insurance.
His grades improved and his teachers began expressing the compliments for which we all hun-
gered. He grew more than four inches in that single
year. My firstborn was maturing into a confident
young man. The driver's license—a bittersweet hur-
dle for me as it is for most parents—welcomed him,
as much as any diploma later would, to his future.*

A Chicken Named America
August 1986

"What do you do with a chicken named America?" the
woman asked. For several years she'd wanted to get rid of
her laying hens but was always stopped by the problem of
what to do with America.

Now, America may look like just another brown and
white hen, but believe me, she is not your average bird. At
the considerable age of 14, equal to at least 100 years in
human terms, she is ancient—for a chicken. America is
evidence of a theory I have: that creatures with unusual
names seem to live longer than others with monikers such
as Rex or Sport. Nowadays chickens are around only long
enough to lay eggs for a year or so until they get turned
into soup or frozen dinners. But, as the woman says, "No
one wants to eat a chicken named America."

During the last few years there were times when
America the chicken began to look peaked. Her comb
drooped, and her feathers molted at the wrong time of the
year. "Something's got to be done about America," the

67

woman would say to her husband. Whereupon the hen would immediately spring back to life, even going so far as to lay an occasional egg.

Like most creatures of longevity, America is smart and stubborn. She can be arrogant—not the kind of chicken to say "please" and "thank you." It's possible that she learned this attitude from one of her contemporaries on the farm, an ill-mannered Siamese cat appropriately named Madame Bovary, who lived to be 19. To those who would scoff, "What's in a name?" I refer a 39-year-old pony named Lucifer, known to my vet as an ornery creature. Who's to say this sly fellow didn't trade on his name and sell his soul for a go-now, pay-later deal?

It is a fact that children are responsible for some of the most unusual names given to family pets. My brother and I always named our animals after people we'd read about in books or characters in the cartoons we saw between movies at the Circle theatre. We had a cat named Sylvester, who lounged about feasting sumptuously on table scraps—awakening only now and then to lick his chops — and lived to be old and fat. Another, dubbed Sebastian, my mother refused to call lest the neighbors think her given to obscenities.

One of the most enjoyable stories I've ever covered as a journalist was of a 32-year-old duck named Katrina. Although her name was Eastern European, Katrina did not eat yogurt as did famous Russian centenarians. She lived on Purina Dog Chow and cracked corn and passed away at 33. Her owners, too, had other long-lived animals with eccentric names. There was Mao Tse Tung, an immense longhaired tiger cat, and Negus, a black cat named for the emperor of Abyssinia. Both lived to be 20.

Added to these venerable animals are other aged notables with memorable names: Remus the basset hound, who was predeceased by his brother, Romulus; Petunia the cat; Clarence, a female Afghan hound; Massa, the world's oldest gorilla; and Wildfire, a local mare who was still being ridden until the year before she died at age 45.

Most ironic, however, are Adam and Eve, a pair of piranhas bought in the 1950s—when it was still legal to sell the fish—by a high school student. Although these carnivores aren't supposed to live long in captivity, the young man became so attached to the fish that he carried them with him when he went away to college. Likewise, they went along when he became a biology teacher and when he got married. He even went to the five-and-dime store to buy goldfish for their suppers. And when he and his wife had children, the first thing they taught the kids was to keep their fingers out of the piranha tank. Finally, on the move to a new job in New Jersey, this fellow packed his piranhas in a plastic bag just as he'd done many times before. But this time, in a fit of petulance, Eve bit a hole in the bag and they both died.

Goldfish aside, my vet says that, like us, animals live longer if they are lean. Don't feed them too much canned dog food, give them bulk, "keep 'em skinny," he told me, relating a story about a California researcher who raised the oldest living mouse in the world. The mouse ate for five days and fasted for two, according to his keeper. "He was a skinny-looking guy, too," laughs my vet.

I must admit that there are a few exceptions to these theories about names and diet. One of them is a very old cow kept by a neighbor of the woman who owns America. When this cow stopped producing milk some years back, her owner put her in a box stall where she has been eating royally ever since. "Been meanin' to take her to market," the man says. A nice round ton, the cow is as fat as she is long. Her coat is shiny and her eyes, bright. She's been around so long that the man can't remember just how old she is. And she doesn't even have a name.

As it turns out, the man has agreed to take his neighbor's flock of chickens—including America. Although he never names any of his farm animals, he seems to like the idea of inheriting this chicken. "Yep," he smiles, "America looks like she's good for a couple of years yet."

After a period of having to settle for store-bought eggs, I once again have the luxury of a friend nearby with a small, free-range flock of Rhode Island Reds who each lay at least one egg a day. None of them is anywhere near as old as America.

I Keep a Horse
August 1986

I don't smoke, drink or run around with loose men. I keep a horse. The horse was acquired from my 14-year-old son, Lisle, in the same manner that most parents acquire a piano (I have one of those, too): i.e., child wants piano lessons so parents buys piano; child grows disenchanted and parent dusts piano. A horse and a piano weigh each about 1,000 pounds, require a substantial investment and consume much space.

However, the piano neither eats hay nor produces any byproducts.

Not that I was looking for an addition to my list of responsibilities on what I had affectionately but realistically dubbed "Falling-Down Farm," a 21-acre backache with farm house and outbuildings in a never-ending state of disrepair.

There were already enough mouths to feed: two steers with a knack for walking through fences; five sheep, including a ram that held the world's record for causing broken tailbones; an old goat named Pansy; three pigs the kids swore the dog had taught to bark; five cats that consumed 60 pounds of fish-flavored cat food every month and one mouse every two months; and a lazy dog who refused to bark. Why should he bark now that we had barking pigs?

Bunny seemed the perfect animal. The color of a copper penny, she was an 18-year-old crossbreed with a friendly disposition and no bad habits. Though she'd been a brood mare for the last seven years and was somewhat pot-bellied, she turned into Cinderella when she entered the ring.

My son saw her, and it was love at first ride. Within a month the romance was wearing thin. Lovers weren't supposed to muck out stalls and pick hooves, and horse manure was a bit disenchanting. Other fascinations appeared on the scene. First it was football after school with the guys, then basketball and wrestling. And girls. Then Lisle fell from a friend's horse and was dragged, foot stuck in the stirrup, for a quarter mile. Before long, I found myself trudging to the barn every morning and night.

"So you got yourself a horse," the neighbors observed. "Lot of work, isn't it?" My farming community saw horses go out when tractors came in, and animals that don't turn into steaks or lay eggs are considered the same sort of profligate luxury as kept women with automatic dishwashers (I have one of those, too).

By all appearances, Bunny was as useless as a spinet standing out there in the meadow. But I liked the horse, so I fed, cleaned and groomed her. I marveled at how different she was from the other animals. It wasn't just her smell—a sweet, furry odor—or her intelligence. It was the communication between us. She was the only farm animal I'd ever had that, when I grew to love her, loved me back.

I bought boots and a hard hat and had a riding lesson on her once a week. We were just working up from the walk to the sitting trot when the harmony turned to dissonance.

One sunny morning, I fell through the barn floor and broke my back.

"Sell the horse," my pragmatic husband advised.

"Get rid of her, Mom," said my fickle younger child as I slogged around the house in a corset-size body cast. Getting my back in shape to get on Bunny's back became my ambition. It was a long, hot summer, but the cast finally came off. I began exercising, readying myself for more lessons.

Then Bunny came up lame. Now it was her turn to hobble.

A friend had cautioned me that the cheapest thing I would do with a horse was to buy it. He was right. When the vet handed me the bill, I knew why this was called the sport of kings.

My horse was, it turned out, nothing more than a 1,000-pound baby. As I bent over the hurt foot and carried buckets of warm saltwater, she leaned on me like a sick kid. I used her bottle of Absorbine Jr. on my aching back at night and listened to my husband complain.

We hibernated through winter until good weather arrived and Bunny and I were feeling chipper. We even had a few riding lessons before the spring rains came.

One wet morning, the normally robust Bunny was off her feed. While I scraped mud from her molting winter coat, she hung her head and spiked a fever. There were antibiotic injections to give and medicines to add to her feed. She had the flu.

This time I paid the vet off with grocery money and hid the bill in the bottom of my lingerie drawer.

"*When* are you going to sell that horse?" my husband asked for the dozenth time.

He was right, of course. Selling her was the practical thing to do. But I thought of those big brown eyes, and the warm velvet nose with its graying whiskers. Bunny had a lot of good years left.

I knew that if I didn't keep her she had maybe one more stop as an old brood mare before she went to the auction block or, worse, the meat packers. Besides, there was no telling when we might both feel like fillies again...

It took two years for us to find the right buyer—the wife of a local farrier—for Bunny, and it broke my heart to see her go. The last I heard, she'd continued to function as a school horse and lived into old age. When I think of her inimitable spirit, I can still recall that sweet, horsy smell.

Unfinished Sonata in Cast Iron
November 1994

A bathtub sits in my living room. It's nice—cast iron, white and quite heavy as bathtubs go. My husband brought it home in the bed of his pickup truck; I am delighted to have it and have told him so.

It's been a long time coming, this bathtub. For 15 years or more, my husband has been contemplating finishing our upstairs bathroom. When our children were small, he got the idea to install a new bath in an unused bedroom so we could avoid the early morning crush. He ripped up floorboards and ripped out the old horsehair plaster, soldered water lines and installed drainpipes. Upstairs and down he ran, checking for leaks each time a section of pipe was completed.

Finally we had a working sink—a good-condition, genuine antique pedestal sink, thank you—that had been pieced together from no fewer than four sets of vintage porcelain pedestals and basins found at yard sales and auctions in various states of disrepair. It was joined, if not complemented, by a brand new toilet and Fiberglass bathtub complete with glass shower doors.

And we were able to use our new extra bathroom—despite the fact that our well-intentioned head of household never completely finished it.

Plaster and paint never went up on the drywall I had spackled. Molding never found its way around the windows and doors. The hole where a medicine chest was supposed to be never held medicine, and the bones of a linen closet never stored linens.

Oh, he intended to finish it, he truly did. He just never got around to it. There was always something more pressing, you see. Something else that required his attention in the way things will for the man of the house.

The boys wanted to build a fort, the pasture required fence posts, or the garden needed tending and, before you knew it, it was time to cut the Christmas tree. Soon the boys were begging for a basketball hoop, our field corn required harvesting, it was time to change the oil in the tractors, and then, wouldn't you know, it was time to cut the Christmas tree. Eventually, the boys wanted to learn to drive, and that was the year the roof needed patching and, of course, it was time to put up the Christmas tree. Then, just a few years ago the boys went away to college during the very same years that the garage needed cleaning and the house roof needed patching again.

I suspected that finishing projects was against his religion.

What religion is that, you might ask.

Everyman's religion.

You see, my husband is a wonderful person—sensitive, intelligent, affectionate and even romantic in his own way. Yet, like most men, he has one aggravating flaw, a trait that—much as I love him—drives me crazy. A failing that in this day and age might be considered grounds for justifiable homicide.

He loves starting things but he has little interest in finishing them.

I think it has something to do with feeling needed. As long as the projects remain unfinished, he has no reason to feel redundant. Like a survivor of some great conflict, he has work that must be finished, work that only he can complete (certainly, no self-respecting contractor would take over *this* project). As long as the bathroom sits there waiting, he is necessary.

If this man had a theme song, it would be "The Unfinished Sonata." Often I imagine him at 99, flashing a toothless smile at the grim reaper and shouting, "Not now—I haven't finished the upstairs bathroom yet."

It's comforting, however, to observe the way time takes care of some things. When we installed the first bathtub, I wanted a cast iron model. You know, the kind you can sink into after a long day's work to soak in bubbles up to your chin. The kind that wraps itself around you and beckons you to read the first volume of *War and Peace* with your head propped on a waterproof pillow. But cast iron seemed expensive then, so we bought one of the ubiquitous Fiberglass models on which the finish readily yellowed and aged during the next 15 years.

So when he asked what I wanted for our 30th wedding anniversary, I told him, "a new bathtub and a finished bathroom."

Now I have a new cast iron bathtub sitting in my living room. It's quite nice as bathtubs go. I've waited a long time for this tub and I'm very glad to have it.

If only I could get in it and take a bath.

The cast iron bathtub was installed and our upstairs bathroom was finished in 1995.

Chapter 3
Root Stock and Scions
❧

In the nature versus nurture debate, I am a living example of how we can be transformed by both place and people. So much about the people I interviewed in this unique geography was colorfully new to me and unusual in the outside world. I was learning by example from individuals at the opposite end of the spectrum from me in philosophy, assimilating their practical wisdom and applying it to my own life in a variety of areas, making deposits in a well of information that I could draw from in times of adversity. Most importantly I began to recognize that I would benefit more from listening—to people, plants and animals—than from talking.

Early on, my friend Teeta Daniels introduced me to Mary Starner, the first subject in this chapter; for this kindness and many others I am forever in Teeta's debt. Among the things I learned from Mary was the enterprising way early mothers measured their children's physical progress with a piece of string, not so different from the aforementioned formula our farm neighbors used to gauge the growth of livestock. Irene Starner, Mary's daughter, also taught me by her own good example never to use the word *can't*. "What's Irene going to do?" people in the Goodyear area asked after her mother and father died, leaving Irene alone in her wheelchair. Irene did just fine, as it turned out, living on her own in the house she'd known since childhood and continuing to crank up the old wood-fired Monarch cook stove, especially at Christmas when she baked hundreds of cookies as gifts for others along with a "Happy Birthday, Jesus" cake for Teeta's family.

Ironstone Woman
August 1989

Mary Starner was a tart old woman. When I met her, she'd been blinded by cataracts for ten years and walked only those places she could get to by leaning on the back of her daughter's wheelchair. Laser surgery failed to cut the problem from her eyes, but the disappointment didn't dull her sense of humor.

A shiny four-quart teakettle always sputtered on the cookstove in the Starners' house. Beneath the Insulbrick siding, the walls were thick chestnut logs; the windows were wrinkly hand-poured glass. Residential dwellings erupted here and there, and over the hill a housing development threatened the boundaries of the 46-acre farm the Starners had bought in 1941. Eventually, the houses filled with average American families. They passed Mary's house and never knew she lived there.

Inside, Mary sat on a platform rocker with a sweater spread over her lap. She'd cock her silver head from side to side, seeing with her ears, listening for faces of friends who stopped to visit. At 79, she could see only light and dark, yet never a shadow darkened her independence. She headed an average American family of days gone by, when wages were a dollar a day, when people doctored their own, and when welfare money had a stigma that kept proud people hungry.

Today, there's nothing average about Mary's family.

"Pop's my legs and Mom's eyes," her 55-year-old daughter, Irene, would say. Irene has been resigned to a wheelchair since her back was broken in a haying accident 35 years ago. Howard, her father, developed heart trouble at "eighty-couple" of years, she said. Together, the three of them did the laundry, cooked the meals, gardened, canned and cleaned—independent, yet totally interdependent, each with her or his own work. Irene cooked and baked and paid the bills. Howard tidied the house and hung out wash. Mary snapped string beans, shelled peas and mixed her recipes for dandelion wine and homemade salve. They had no time cards to punch, no social calendars to keep, no Mastercard or Visa. In a time when family suppers became a rare occurrence, the Starners knew each other with a kind of intimacy lost by the "Me" generation.

"Been married 56 years," said Mary, "and never got a penny of welfare. Raised two children—they're Depression babies—and to this day, the only bills we got comin' is telephone and electric."

Mary was a folk healer, known locally for her ability to "cure for" various ailments. "It's all common sense," she used to tell me. The cures were passed on to her by a hobo in return for help she offered during the hard times of the 1930s. "Poverty House, we called that place," said Mary of the shanty she and Howard occupied when the man knocked on their door asking for a drink from the pitcher pump out back. A rich man ruined by the stock market crash, he'd come here looking for work in the fruit orchards. He learned the remedies when he took to the road. "Every time he came by, I'd give him coffee and he'd tell me one or two things," she said.

What she got from him was a cultivation of the innate sense of independence everyday people possessed in the days when babies were born at home and most folks never saw the inside of a hospital even when they were dying. And, though there were several biblical incantations that went along with the applications of some, his potions weren't as much magic as practical remedies for people who either couldn't afford a doctor or get to one.

"A corner of bread will stop bleeding from a cut," she said: "Bread's the staff of life." Ezekiel 16:6 is said over the victim of an effusive nosebleed: "And when I passed by thee, and saw thee polluted in thine own blood, I said unto thee 'When thou [here, she repeats the person's name three times] was't in thy blood. Live.' Yea, I said unto thee, 'When thou [repeat the name three times] was't in thy blood. Live.' " Mary's Bible was always marked at appropriate places with birthday cards and memorials.

She used common therapies such as witch hazel for bruises, jewel weed for poison ivy, and an onion cut in half for warts. She rubbed the onion on the wart, then planted the onion.

Fire could be removed from burns, she claimed, by reciting the following: "Fire burn us. Water quenches thirst. God's free will passes by," and blowing over the burn. "If you don't put water or nothin' on it, the burn'll never blister," said Mary, provided the sufferer did not take the Lord's name in vain when it happened. "Don't swear when you burn yourself, won't nothin' work." Mary performed this on a woman when she worked at a nearby apple processing plant in her younger days. Scalding applesauce had spilled on her frantic coworker, but she reportedly didn't have a mark when Mary was done with her. Mary claimed the ability to work this cure could be passed from a man to a woman who'd borne a child and vice versa but not to a person of the same sex.

A few years ago she was called on to lecture a class of cultural anthropology students at Dickinson College in Carlisle. She'd go, she told the professor, provided the students really wanted to listen and wouldn't laugh at her. Mary got dressed up in a hat and Sunday clothes, though, "truth be known," she offered, she didn't often go to church.

"I went to the third grade and that's all the farther," she began, telling the story of her cures and offering old-fashioned advice while the students sat, enthralled. When the class was finished at twice the planned-for time, they asked thoughtful, serious questions, taking notes and never patronizing or demeaning her.

"You don't plant lima beans until the locust trees blossom," Mary told them. And if you cut your hair in the increase of the moon, "you're gonna get hair in a hurry." Yet, if you wait until the moon is on the wane, you can go without a haircut for several months.

She passed out recipes for some of her remedies, including hobo salve.

Hobo Salve

Take equal parts—"if it's a pound, make 'em all a pound"— of tallow, rosin, beeswax and unsalted butter. Boil the ingredients in a heavy pot—"one you don't want no more"—until well blended. There will be sediment in the bottom—don't mind this.

Use for cuts, boils and scratches. Very good for bed sores.

Not so very long ago, a young child's failure to thrive was a grave concern among parents. Marked by weight loss, the condition was called slow growth or "flesh decay." Mary's test for the worrisome diagnosis was as follows: "If a child ain't growin', take a piece of lappin' yarn [string] and measure from his heel to the top of his head [and cut it]. Take the same piece of lappin' yarn and, startin' from his heel, wind it up to the big toe and round his heel again and round and round till it's all. If it comes out seven [seven times the length of his foot], then he don't have flesh decay."

The child who failed to measure up was bathed in a warm tea made from boiling wild snapdragon leaves and flowers. He "might look a little green," attested Irene, based on her own childhood experience, "but it don't hurt."

In fact, the good in Mary's cures seems to be that they didn't hurt. The sufferer was soothed by the fact that someone was concerned about his poor health and going to a lot of trouble to determine a cause. The physical benefit of all this positive thought and good faith surely must have given a boost to his immune system, and the dash of mystery probably didn't hurt, either.

"Pass it on," Mary always told folks to whom she gave the cures. My friend Teeta Daniels, a neighbor of the Starners, says her favorite of these homespun remedies is one for earache. "Pee on a piece of cotton and put it in your ear," Mary instructed. Presumably there was some efficacy in having something warm next to the ache.

Before she lost her sight, Mary would go out every fall to gather boneset, sassafras, horsemint, dittany and pennyroyal for herbal teas that were used to treat everything from diarrhea to constipation. And in springtime, when people in housing developments were calling Chemlawn to poison the dandelions in their yards, she was harvesting them. "A dandelion's one thing God made that you can use every inch of it," she claimed. The leaves provide salad greens, the roots can be ground for coffee, and some people ferment the blossoms for dandelion wine. Her recipe for sweet dandelion wine is famous among old timers in the neighborhood.

Dandelion Wine

Mix one full quart dandelion blossoms with one gallon of water in a kettle on the cook stove.
Add slices of one lemon, unpeeled, and two and one-half pounds of sugar.
Boil five minutes, then cool.
Add two tablespoons of good yeast.
Keep the mixture in a crock in a warm place three days or till it ferments, then strain.
Bottle and cork tightly.

Use only for medicinal purposes. Good for diarrhea.

Mary liked to tell the story of a neighbor who seemed to be consuming her dandelion wine at a rapid rate: "I asked her, 'How often do you get sick?' 'Oh, every evening at about 5 o'clock,' she said."

Mary's mind held a solution for every problem. If your dog ran away, she'd advise you to go to the barn or any outbuilding that had a knothole. You were then to call the dog's name through the hole nine times, followed by the phrase "come home."

"If the dog is tied or penned, he'll come home as soon as he gets away," she'd say. "If he's with a lady friend, he'll come back soon as his job's done." Shorty Taylor's dog was found this way—he came home all the way from Arendtsville.

The Starner family's prized possession was a delicate old satin-muslin quilt, a museum-quality piece of handwork. When her mother gave it to her, she told Mary the top was 75 years old.

"Just rub your hand over it and feel it," Irene marveled the day she showed it to me. The iridescent silky white fabric was picked with exquisite hand stitching, eight stitches to the half inch, in tiny half-inch squares. Around its octagonal center was a detailed thistle design with row upon row of trailing flowers and a garland border. It was a wedding dress for a bed.

Irene kept the quilt in her cedar chest but said she would pass it along to her brother Byron's eldest son one day. She told me she had no regrets about her life. The accident and the wheelchair had given her an appreciation of commonplace things she would not have noticed otherwise, and she'd become closer to her mother. Mary put her daughter to work, never gave her time for self-pity. She'd had a lot better bringing-up than most of the young folks in the rows of houses over the hill, Irene reckoned. "Ya' know, kids today got memories, but they're bought memories. I've got lots of memories."

Unable to get the rosin in quantity, I have never made Mary's hobo salve, but my friend Margaret Brandt picked quantities of dandelion blossoms in the spring of 2007 and adapted Mary's recipe for a less sweet version of her dandelion wine. Uncorked, it had a healthy kick, the bouquet of fresh spring dandelions and the taste of a piquant chardonnay.

The Talisman
June, 1984

She sat there fingering the photograph, staring at it with such intensity that the young woman pictured might have walked right off the Kodak paper and into the labor camp kitchen.

Smiling and curly-haired, the girl was the eldest of her six children. The picture was of her high school graduation. It must have been how she, herself, looked at 18.

Now her hands were hardened with the harvests of apples and citrus, but her clear, olive-skinned face showed few signs of weariness except for mauve circles around the black-brown eyes.

The woman was an illegal immigrant. In 1979 she was smuggled into this country in the back of a pickup truck. It cost her $800, money hard-saved after paying hospital bills for her young son. More than a year ago she was apprehended in a nighttime raid on a central Pennsylvania labor camp and sent back to Mexico by immigration officials. She returned to this country within a week and thereafter slept outside at night with her three-year-old daughter in fear of being deported again.

"Why does she do it?" I asked through a Mexican-American interpreter.

"The reason she is here is because in Mexico she cannot make a decent living. She is a widow, and in Mexico you just can't make enough money to feed your children and give the education," the interpreter said.

In Mexico, her five older children live with her aged mother, she explained. Since her father is also dead, she supports all of them. Other members of the large family depend on her help as well.

When he was four, her oldest son developed polio. The local doctor said he could do nothing for the child, so she took him from their rural village to Mexico City. There she got a job as a maid in a wealthy household and worked for the Mexican equivalent of $20 a month to pay for a total of 12 operations on her son's legs. Without help from the woman for whom she worked, she said, she couldn't have paid off the debt. It was in Mexico City that she first saw life without poverty and learned the value of education. There, she determined to change life for her children.

I looked at the little almond-eyed three-year-old, runny-nosed with a cold. Her mother coughed, and I asked how they managed the cold fall nights sleeping outside.

"The reason she does it is the fear...It is hard work. She is killing herself," our translator observed.

The woman hesitated, then answered in a soft rush of Spanish: "You feel humiliated, you feel it deep in your heart. But you don't have a choice. What you want is for your children to have a choice."

The fear, I realized, was not for her own safety, but that her children might have to live as she did. She is only one among millions of illegal aliens who have crossed U.S. borders in search of work.

Figures on the number of illegals entering the U.S. vary from source to source, but it is obvious that the complexion of cities and towns near our agricultural centers is rapidly changing as Mexicans flee poverty in their homeland, poverty brought about in part, according to the Mexican president, by high U.S. interest rates.

With the peso greatly reduced in value, it's a good time for Americans to visit Mexico, but immigration reform may soon make it a bad time for Mexicans to "visit" the U.S.

Last fall Charles Kuralt, in one of his CBS-TV *Sunday Morning* broadcasts, discussed the problem of illegal immigration. Two young men interviewed had traveled from deep within Mexico's interior, Kuralt said, to work and study in the U.S.

Said one of them: "This is the only country where there is any hope. When there is no longer hope in your country, where you are afraid you will die, you will do anything to hope." They were caught and returned by the border patrol.

As I interviewed the woman, I wondered if immigration reform really could expect to kill such hope. At the risk of being caught, she returned to her home again last summer to see her daughter graduate and to have her little girl christened. While they were there, the three-year-old got sick with diarrhea, quickly dehydrated and lost more than 10 pounds.

"There is no clinic there to take kids to," the interpreter explained. "The first thing a doctor in Mexico asks is, 'Do you have money?'"

An American friend paid for their safe return to the U.S.

I asked the woman what she wanted for herself. She smiled and said that her future didn't mean anything. "I don't want to die or get sick till all of my kids go to school and get a job. After that, I'm ready to lay down." She is 43.

"What about free time?" I pressed. "What would she do if she could have time for whatever she wanted?"

She laughed, answering through the interpreter. "Without working, I cannot live. We can't afford to have free time. Free time is something that we hate."

In Mexico, it is no small accomplishment to finish high school. The woman's greatest source of pride was that her daughter had won a scholarship and was now going to a college. She rubbed the picture and looked at it again, longingly. It seemed her most prized possession—a talisman.

In 1988, I wrote another column in which I felt freer to use the name of this woman, Ricarda, who I hoped would never have to hide again. At that time, implementation of the Immigration Reform and Control Act of 1986 promised to address many problems of illegal aliens, especially the farmworkers so badly needed in our fruit-growing region. However, illegal immigration has become a much larger and more complicated issue nationwide. Close to my home, the village of York Springs is sometimes disparagingly called "Little Mexico."

Something to Keep Goin'
October 1985

"Sweet Cider," announce faded signs on either side of John Wirt's fruit stand. Trucks on local business whiz along the old road to Gettysburg, sending swirling autumn leaves in their wake. Cars seldom stop these days. But familiar customers return to the little stand, drawn by bright colors of Indian corn, dried yarrow and pumpkins reflecting the glow of autumn sunlight from behind the weathered wooden siding. They come back to the man who dispenses stories with his cider and always has time to talk.

A smartly dressed young woman steers her Chevy hatchback off the road. "I'd like some of that sweet cider," she says.

Wirt pronounces it "side-er," with the first syllable drawn out and gives her a three-minute history of cider presses from the days when apples were squeezed through burlap sacks to modern times of hydraulic presses and stainless steel tanks.

"I'm so thirsty for cider," she bubbles. She tells him she's not from around here, noting that her grandfather makes cider. Like the old customers, she is thirsty for stories, too. Wirt gathers his pride and tells her his is the only stand left where cider is sold in glass jugs. He no longer presses his own but takes his jugs to a local cider mill for filling: eight plastic, four glass. This cider has no preservatives and should be stored in the refrigerator with the lid slightly unscrewed.

Several of his customers won't drink cider from a plastic jug, he says. "Don't know what they'd do if I wasn't around...I will admit, though, cider right from the press tastes better in glass. Very seldom do I drink cider out of a plastic jug."

"Come back," he offers. "Cider's always in the 'friger-ator." He makes change from a worn cigar box, packing her cider and a dollar's worth of gourds in recycled paper bags. "I will," she replies, smiling and promising to return his jug when she comes this way again. "I don't have near the business I used to have, but I don't want it," Wirt observes, settling his spare, gray frame into a folding chair. "Because, after all, when you're 81 years old, you gotta slow down....No, I'm doin' pretty good for bachin' it for seven years." His wife died seven years ago, he explains.

"My wife told me good advice before she passed away. She said, 'Keep the fruit stand goin' as long as you're able, it'll give you something to do and you'll get people to talk to.' And she said, 'Make yourself good things to eat, because you're a good cook.' But she never dreamt that the prices of peaches and apples would get to where they are today.

"To be honest with you, I ain't makin' anything." He buys most of his fruit from a local orchard but doesn't sell much, he admits. "A lot of my customers are my neighbors and people that's been here before and keeps comin' back And I try to stay as near reasonable as I can. But I know I ain't makin' any profit. Like my wife said, it's somethin' to do, somethin' to keep goin'."

Wirt tells me he grew up in the house just a stone's throw away: "I been here since I was six weeks old, except a year and a half when I first got married." He has two children, four grandchildren, and 11 great-grandchildren.

Across the way grow shellbark hickory trees, the progeny of two old trees his children gathered nuts from; their leaves glow orange-gold against the blue autumn sky. A long line of daffodils borders old Route 15 here and blooms in a yellow roadside ruffle every spring. Next to it he used to plant chrysanthemums to sell in the fall: "I never planted less than a thousand, all different colors...and that field was beautiful. People used to stop and take pictures."

He's had the fruit stand for 20 years. "I was lookin' to retire from the carpenter business," he says, "so I built a couple a' chicken houses." When he couldn't get a reasonable wholesale price for his eggs, he set them out on a bench next to a pear tree in his yard. "First day, I didn't sell an egg, and my wife laughed at me. Second day, I sold eggs. Third day, I put tomatoes out. And from then on, I kept on goin'....One thing I know helped me along—I don't smoke, chew nor drink.

"Oh, I know it's really not safe for me to be here by myself anymore, but I'm gonna' stick it out," he declares from under the permanent OPEN sign nailed to the overhang. "I was robbed once't." The thief broke down his doors and stole the little he had worth taking but couldn't steal his spirit.

"No use for me to set and worry...I just take each day the way it comes. Anyway, I'm still here.

"Come back," he says. "Cider's always in the 'frigerator."

John Wirt's fruit stand is long gone, but his row of daffodils blooms every spring in a yellow ruffle along old Route 15.

Ike Beam, Beekeeper
November 1986

Ike Beam is a hunter, fisher, tobacco chewer and beekeeper. He wears an impeccably trimmed white toothbrush moustache that gives him the aura of a British butler—until he speaks. His is the nasal banjo twang of folks who live in the hills near Peach Glen.

"I've been so busy gettin' these bees down b'fore the end of the month," he says, "for I'm leavin' then for Potter County for an indefinite st-a-a-y." Ike has the habit of drawing out the last syllable of every sentence, slow as honey pours in January, punctuating the whole thing with a smile and a twinkling eye.

It is a blue-skyed, orange-leafed autumn morning as we walk in to one of his beeyards, which he calls an "out-yard," on the Pennsylvania State Game Lands. All got up in a pith helmet, bee veil and heavy long-sleeved gloves, I am a bit nervous as Ike lifts his veil to spit some tobacco juice and tells me bee stings are just a hazard of the occupation. The trick is to keep loose areas of clothing buttoned up, he says, because the bees like to crawl into the warm folds of sleeves, pant legs and armpits when the weather turns cool.

Ike and his friend Sam Bolen are gathering the last of the season's honey today and getting their hives ready for winter. Together, they have 665 beehives, most of them Sam's. Ike says he is gradually getting out of the bee business: "I've got a lot of huntin' and fishin' to catch up on." Sam says Ike taught him everything he knows.

We tramp over red leaves of poison ivy and Virginia creeper to get to the hives. In this area the nectar flow comes from wild asters, Ike reveals, pointing to a sea of fuzzy white blooms that provide game cover in the adjacent fields. The taste and color of honey is determined by the nectar flow in the surrounding area, he says, and I recall that a few years ago he sold me some locust honey—wonderfully perfumed and light in color—after a spring of heavy locust bloom.

In the bright autumn sunshine, Sam pronounces these hives warm enough to open, noting that air temperature must reach 45 degrees for bees to start flying. He walks toward us carrying a smoking metal contraption with a bellows on its side and a top like a funnel. "I wouldn't work without a smoker," he says. Lifting the lid to show me a piece of smelly, smoldering burlap inside he says the idea is to encourage some of the field force (workers) to get out so there aren't quite as many bees left inside the hive to sting the beekeeper.

Ike continues his work. "It doesn't hurt the bees none. We blow smoke on them and they sit back and rub their eyes. Then we can go to work.

"Bees aren't the vicious creatures you think they are," he declares as Sam checks the supers, topmost in the beehives. "Somebody'd come in my house this time of year and rob my grub out, I'm afraid I'd get madder 'n what they are."

Each hive is different, some stronger and more productive than others, depending on their populations, numbering from 50,000 to 100,000 bees per hive. Some are short of honey, and Sam and Ike replenish their spare supers with full racks from the more affluent hives. Ike characterizes bees as individuals. Like people, some are docile, others are ill-tempered, he says, puffing the smoker at the door of the first hive.

"They have a very highly civilized structure—more than we're aware of. They've been here a couple of million years, and we've only been here a short while." Beehives have the oldest known form of air conditioning, he tells me, explaining that worker bees carry water and fan their wings to cool the hive in summer. And bees communicate, directing each other to specific sources of nectar miles away. Workers in the field live for only six weeks during the nectar-gathering season; during this time, they literally beat their wings to pieces. Their flying days over, they simply walk out of the hive and die.

The two men winterize each wooden bee house by venting the roofs and feeding the bees with a mixture of granulated sugar and antibiotic powder to protect against disease. We stand in front of the last of several dozen hives as Sam reaches down to flick a bee from my pant leg with a deft motion. Both men have been stung twice today with no ill effects. The sun is warm. The air is thick with bees and alive with a buzzing din. One bee looks for an opening in the netting near my ear as I myopically check the veil for holes, my nose twitching, skin itching. Not to worry. According to Ike, the thing to use on bee stings is honey. It also works on burns and all manner of hurts. I tell the bee man I use honey and lemon juice for coughs, and he gives me his recipe for sore throats. One part honey to one part whiskey, "preferably Jim Beam," he advises in his Peach Glen twang.

But between two of the racks in this hive is a bonus, an extra comb filled with honey. Gently prying, Sam and Ike remove the waxy chambers intact and put the whole oozing comb in a plastic bag that they present to me with a warning to close it quickly before the bees come to recoup their stolen goods. With one short, luscious whiff, my twitching nose is calmed by a symphony of weed and wildflower aromas.

Later, when Ike Beam and his toothbrush moustache have gone after bigger game on their extended stay in Potter County, I will remember this day. I will bake thick white biscuits, take them hot from the oven and spread their steaming middles with the stuff in this comb. As the amber liquid drips into my mouth, I will thank Ike Beam and his bees for the sweet taste of summer.

The first time I met Ike Beam was after a snowfall followed by an ice storm. I picked my way gingerly over the knee-high, glassy crust from the road to his house, where he waited with the door thrown open to his basement workshop, a warm fire roaring in the wood stove.

*"I figure the good lord put it there, the good lord
will take it away," Ike drawled, informing me that
a person "could have a heart attack" shoveling
snow.*

Deer Hunter
November 1986

It was 4 a.m. when I found my youngest in the
kitchen. He scared me, sitting there in the dark, all
dressed up in florescent orange, gun at his side. It would
be a long wait until his father arose in an hour—an even
longer wait for the dawn of the first day of his first deer
season.

Lisle was 13 then. Someone else got the big buck in
the hollow that year, and in the time that followed he
grew disgruntled. His father insisted on precautions and
strict adherence to the rules: no taking off school for hunting, and no hunting doe. We didn't own a 4-wheel-drive
vehicle and had no light for the pre-season practice of
"spotting."

He had yet to get his deer.

Surely babies had been switched in the delivery room,
our second-born thought. Somehow Fate had become con-
fused and placed him on the wrong doorstep.

Now he is 15. This year things will be different, he tells
me. He will travel north to the big woods with his father.
He will sleep in a log cabin that smells of pine and creosote.
He will awaken in the morning to a man-cooked breakfast
and wait in the dark with a hundred other hunters.

I will wait at home and worry, for I am an outsider in
these parts—a mother, an uninvited guest on his journey
into manhood.

In the bathroom now are his razor and shaving cream.
He hides them when I come snooping. He laughs his qua-

vering, double-register adolescent laugh. Part of him wants to linger in childhood; part of him wants that child to skip away as easily as the would-be whiskers wash down the sink drain.

Plans for the hunting trip have been intricately laid. For months he's studied stacks of *Outdoor Life* and *Field and Stream* magazines where the centerfolds of his fantasies wear antlers, not bikinis. He's talked incessantly of strategies, tree stands, guns and ammunition. Now, in the middle of a discussion about Algebra homework, his eyes glaze, triggered by some smell or sound, and his head is occupied with the hunt.

"Hey, Dad," he shouts to the man sitting just beside him. "I'm gonna try that sex stuff.

Hands on hips, I protest. "Sex stuff? Now, wait a minute!"

"Don't worry, Mom. It's for deer…First you take a bath in baking soda. Then you wash all your clothes in baking soda."

"Doesn't sound very sexy to me," I counter. The thought of his voluntarily doing his own laundry in baking soda or anything else is ludicrous to me; however, I obviously am not included in the conversation.

"Then you set this stuff out in canisters all around you. It's sex attractant. S'posed to smell real good to the deer. One a' the guys tried it last year. Said the deer came right up to him, but they were the wrong kind. Used the stuff to attract buck when it was doe season, and not a single lady deer came near him."

"Humph," I mutter, relieved no would-be mother had been shot. It is forever foreign to me: the hunt, the wait, the adrenaline and sweat, the stop-your-heart sight of the velvet beast, the aim—and then the shot. A game warden once explained hunting to me in terms of a metamorphosis. First the boy shoots just to make sure his gun works, the warden said, and he takes aim at everything in sight.

Soon, he equates good hunting with numbers and wants to bag his limit. But as he matures, one elusive animal may capture the hunter's attention, and he is consumed by observing the habits and psychology of this solitary creature. The final phase occurs when the hunter, at one with nature, successfully tracks his prey and chooses, at the exact moment of the potential kill, to let it go.

It is a Stone Age rite in the age of the suburban super market. The necessity of the kill is gone but the meta-morphosis of the hunt hangs on. I try to convince myself of its enduring significance as he packs his woolen socks and thermal underwear.

"I love the smell of the woods," he smiles at me. "I love to hunt."

Yes, he will smell the moldering leaves of the big woods. He will notice wild turkey and bear skat. At night he will go with the men to the mountain hotel where he'll sip birch beer and laugh at the banter of the one-man band and dancing fat lady. He will watch the sun rise through the still-golden leaves of the beech trees. He will wait in the cold for the oh-so-longed-for buck. He may or may not see him, but that is not important.

I will wait at home and sadly rinse the peach fuzz down the sink drain.

Of our two sons, Lisle, the younger, looks most like me. Just four years old when we moved to the farm, he attended Quaker nursery school, where even a pretend finger gun was not allowed, and was a happy, gregarious child. Jack Hershey, then pro-prietor of Hershey's store, a general merchandise mercantile in York Springs that had been in his family for generations, never forgot my buying both of our boys baby dolls in an early effort to broaden their toy-guns-and-trucks play routines. Still, it seemed to me that Lisle grew into puberty wondering why John and I were so different from the parents of his many friends—older, disinclined to let him go out for football, and lacking a platoon of relatives within shouting distance.

Music Man
September 1987

When Tom Jolin talks, he makes music. When he walks, he makes music. When he crafts pieces of maple and mahogany wood into fine stringed instruments, he makes music. And, when he plays those instruments, he makes the most wonderful toe-tapping, knee-raising, head-bobbing, dancing, singing music.

It's "old-timey music," according to Tom. "It's a real fun type of music....You don't have to intellectualize it a lot to enjoy it, you just go ahead and play it." It's been played for centuries by people in the Appalachian hills; and the song of those hills—the look and feel and smell of the old times—sings in the tunk-a-ka-tunk of the banjo and the tinkling of the dulcimer strings.

"I've been musical all my life," Tom tells me. As a kid back home in Wisconsin, he played the baritone horn, "because Uncle Arnie had it and he wasn't using it." He laughs, remembering how his mom wouldn't let him drop band to play baseball full-time in the sixth grade. Later he learned the string bass and performed with various folk groups in college. But it wasn't until he settled in Pennsylvania orchard country that Tom became fully involved in folk music. Here he met the other members of the West Orrtanna String Band, so-called because all the musicians live in the crossroads community of Orrtanna.

Along the way, he taught himself trumpet, banjo, guitar, accordion, harmonica and autoharp. Now his instru-

ment of choice is one he turns out in his own workshop—
the hammer dulcimer.

Tom's dulcimer sits on legs at the end of the dinner
table as he and his wife, Marianne, greet me and my husband on this late summer's eve. Their house is all wood,
in a woods with a clearing toward the south. Here, huge
blue morning glories grow like up-turned tubas on strings
against the windows. Inside are exposed wooden beams
and open wooden stairs festooned with three pajama-clad
children and a big tabby cat.

We hear the rhythm of West Virginia in his Wisconsin
baritone as Tom speaks, "I made this...now I'm learnin' to
play it." He holds up a shiny violin—his first—and treats
us to two fiddle pieces, "I Shall Rise" and "The Yellow
Rose of Texas." Next, he brings out a button accordion and
also plays that for us, knees pumping up and down in time
with the music all the while he pushes the accordion bellows in and out.

Then, having saved the best for last, he sits before the
hammer dulcimer—a fascinating wooden sound box with
wire strings stretched over it. "They're fine instruments,"
Tom says, explaining that they originated in 800 or 900
A.D. in the country we now know as Turkey. Each culture
has its own version of the hammer dulcimer, he says,
mentioning Germany, Greece and China; however, in the
United States, this instrument, which is not related to the
Appalachian lap dulcimer, nearly died out. He picks up
his wooden mallets and breaks into "Temperance Reel"
and then "Simple Gifts." And we can almost smell the Appalachian wildflowers.

Altogether Tom has crafted 19 hammer dulcimers and
has another waiting in his shop right now along with a
guitar he's started "just for the experience." The instrument he plays tonight is clear-toned and beautifully fashioned of birch and mahogany with a cherry border. Two

rosettes, his trademark, are hand carved into the yellow birch top for sound holes; adjacent to them run two maple rails with brass rods, a treble bridge and a bass bridge, and side bridges at either end of the instrument. Across them 58 steel strings stretch in courses, three strings per course for treble and two for bass, in a crisscross pattern. Most dulcimers these days are made with two strings per course, but the first Tom made was modeled after one at the Smithsonian and had 92 strings, four per course.

He prefers birch plywood for top and bottom pieces, judging this material acoustically superior to the traditional spruce and maple. If diagrammed, the bell-like quality of the dulcimer tone would show a gradual ascent, building little by little, and then a quick drop-off. With the quick descent, those crystalline sounds become pleasantly muddled after more than a few notes.

Tom's dulcimers are for sale. Building the instruments and seeing them go to people who enjoy the music gives him as much pleasure as playing.

He hands me the mallets, thin sticks of maple that have been sanded to perfect balance. Timidly I touch them to the strings, and the dulcimer takes over. Set in motion, the mallets reverberate with a rhythm of their own, dancing on the instrument. That happens with the dulcimer. It is an instrument that yields a certain imagery, "a tonal picture," Tom says.

Through the Jolins' open windows, songs of crickets and night birds blend with the strings. Before we leave, Tom plays more songs: "Liberty," "Midnight on the Water," "Soldier's Joy," and others. Most haunting is "Big Fairy Hill, Little Fairy Hill," (*Si Bheag Si Mhor*) written by a blind harpist in sixteenth-century Ireland. All the way home, I hear green hills and fairies, my feet still tapping to the trills and runs.

*According to a posting on the Susquehanna Folk
Music Society website, Tom Jolin has performed on
National Public Radio; he's played for former Vice
President Al Gore, and author and NPR personal-
ity Garrison Keillor.*

Crum's Watch Shop
September 1989

Paul Crum has been repairing watches in Bendersville
for more than 44 years. "Crum's Watch Shop," says the
sign outside his home on South Main Street. He came
back home after World War II, eventually bought the
business from his father, and moved it from North Main
Street, about two blocks away.

"That's where I learned it, you know, and where he
learned it...from his father. Now no one's learning it from
me," he says, a jeweler's loupe cocked to one side of his bifocals.

Outside, the summer day is measured by the humming of cicadas and the chirping of crickets; inside it is
gauged by the ticking of watches and clocks, dozens and
dozens of them, old and new, priceless antiques and
Kmart specials.

The first time I met Crum was after my husband
found a vintage Elgin wristwatch for me at a yard sale.
With its hand-worked gold case and diamond-shaped crystal surrounded by sapphire and diamond chips, it was a
treasure I wore on special occasions—until I pulled the
stem out.

"No charge," said Crum, handing it back across the
counter. The stem wasn't broken, he explained; a tiny
pawl, a device allowing rotation in only one direction, was
simply out of place. It was a fine old piece, he allowed.
While we talked, my husband rummaged in the small

cardboard box labeled "Odds and Ends: $1.50" and found an adjustable metal band for a watch he had at home. Later, Crum replaced a crystal on our son's watch at the whopping cost of $2.50.

He doesn't sell watches any more, he tells me, leaning against an oak and glass case where only a few watchbands and chains for pocket watches are now displayed. "I won't sell what I can't service." Most modern watches have quartz movements, he says, and have to be shipped back to the factory for repair; in his opinion, watch manufacturers "want you to dispose of them and buy a new one." Watches made by reliable companies generations ago, however, he finds intriguing: "They took time to make a quality piece with movements that are beautifully decorated. It's a pleasure to work on those watches."

The bell on the door jangles and a customer walks in.

"Would you take a look at this?" she booms, regaling him with stories of the overtime she's put in because her watch didn't work.

"Worse than no watch at all," Crum agrees. "At least you know you don't know what time it is if you have no watch....A watch that doesn't work is a nuisance." The trouble with her watch is dirt, he tells her at a glance. "Works when I knock it around a bit," she says.

"That's because you're pounding the dirt around." After she exits the shop, he shows me that the proper way to set the balance wheel in motion is to tilt the watch from side to side.

Bong! From behind the counter a clock strikes the hour.

"That's a boisterous one," he laughs. Another chimes mellifluously.

"That one was my grandfather's...it has weights instead of mainsprings." Flowers decorate the clock's Roman-numeraled face; a mirror, etched with age, is below the delicate dial, and the whole encased in a walnut-veneered rectangle.

For every timepiece, Crum tells me, there must be a power source: if that power is a mainspring, the spring is wound tightly and provides the force as it unwinds, turning the wheels of the mechanism. Clocks actually "measure" the time, he instructs, his words as metered as the second hands of the watches hanging on hooks behind him, their work tickets vibrating in time with the ticking.

"When you hear a clock ticking, that's the measuring of time."

Big floor clocks tick once per second because of their long pendulums, but small clocks tick much faster. "Listen to that one," he smiles, placing a gilded Victorian mantel clock on the counter. I lean my ear to the case and hear "tick, tick, tick" in the Lady Isabelle—three ticks per second.

"It's physics!" I cry, knowing it has little to do with science and everything to do with time.

"My dad had a book," Crum smiles. "In the forward it said three things are required for watch repairing: good eyes, steady nerves, and complete control of your temper.

"That last one's the most important: patience. Oh, sometimes things get contemptible, and you have days when nothing goes right...but you hope you don't get too many in a row."

A few years ago Crum retired, more or less, but the shop on Main Street still opens precisely at 8 a.m., three days a week.

Now that Crum's Watch Shop is permanently closed, we have few alternatives to the throw-away timepieces available at Wal-Mart.

Denzil Slusser
May 1991

Denzil Slusser has 40 small American flags on his kitchen table, ready to be placed on the veterans' graves in time for Memorial Day. Members of the VFW drop them off every year, and Denzil puts them up. As president and caretaker of the Mt. Zion Evangelical Lutheran Church Cemetery Association, he's been looking after the old graveyard at the Goodyear church and cemetery for 61 years.

"I was on the church council when they started it." That was in 1930, he says. "They said, 'Denzil here's going to have a lifetime job.'...Well, I guess I have. I mowed [the cemetery] last week." Last month, he celebrated his 94th birthday. Today, at least 100 greeting cards—from friends, family and the offspring of his prodigious family including his 10 children, their 20 children and his 18 great-grandchildren—hang from a mini-clothesline strung across his living room or sit on a sideboard by the door.

The patriarch tells me he's lived in South Dickinson Township all his life except for the first three years he was married: "Never got more than a mile and a half away from home. Can you beat that?

"I was school director for six years, tax collector eight years, and secretary and treasurer of the [township] supervisors for 12 years."

Denzil went to the same one-room school that his parents, his children and two of his grandchildren attended. Chestnut ("CHESS-net," he pronounces it) Ridge School was in nearby Georgetown, Cumberland County. According to Denzil, Georgetown was so-named because two George Starners lived there along with a George Slusser and two George Murtoffs—all within a mile of each other.

"I think I served South Dickinson Township fairly

well," he remarks. "Made an awful lot of friends being tax collector." In addition, he worked for 28 years as a carpet weaver at the former Masland factory in Carlisle and as a highway foreman for 10 years; he was a substitute mail carrier, a beekeeper, and did farm work among other things. He has taught Sunday school since 1924.

He remembers the first telephone in these parts. "They run a telephone line all the way from Carlisle for Bill Adams—lived down here in the big farm by Tabor. They took the line through some cherry trees on my dad's property. I used to climb up on those cherry trees to hear the telephone lines jingling."

Denzil's hearing is still impeccable. He wears no hearing aid—and, by the way, neither does his 92-year-old brother, he tells me—and uses glasses only for reading. Every day he reads the newspaper and the Bible. And he writes. Ever since the first year of his marriage to Maude McKinney, March 10, 1921, more than 70 years ago, Denzil has kept a diary.

"I just thought, I'm gonna' mark it down, what happened every day. And if I want to refer back to anything, I got it," he smiles. "I settled many an argument with it....I went to get a haircut this morning. That'll be in there. It'll be in about you comin' here this evening."

He gets out last year's diary to show me, and I notice that some of the pages are slugged at the top by a word or two in explanation of what happened on that day. Later he tells me about the escalating cost of haircuts. "Seven dollars to get your hair cut: that's ridiculous. My uncle used to cut it for ten cents." And I wonder if today's entry will be slugged "haircuts" or "robbery."

I notice that he mentions the weather almost every day in his entries. "Clear, 30 degrees. Went up in the 40s," on Jan. 9, 1990. "Snow melting. A wonderful day. Shoveled snow. Richard Weidner dug Alice Beam's grave....Fixed stove and started fire." This page is slugged "stove."

The next day, Jan. 10, he wrote, "Mostly cloudy, windy and cold. 30 degrees....Lonely, upset, heartbroken. At Alice Beam's funeral. Snow all but gone. No frost in the ground. Valda [one of his daughters, who lives next door] here. Slept on couch."

I ask him about the loneliness that he mentions on more than one page. "I can't explain. Nobody can tell you till you go through it," he replies, noting that it's been 14 years since his Maude died and, even though his family comes calling every Sunday, it isn't the same. Maude is buried in the cemetery on the hill along with two of his children, a granddaughter and many friends whose names and dates of death he lists on the last pages of his diaries. "Yessum, wonderful friends. I go up there and tramp over top of 'em and mow the grass on top of 'em, and they never say a word to me....Many a night I worked all day, came home, got supper and dug a grave with a lantern....It'll be like home when I go up there."

He'd intended to put the flags in the cemetery today, he says, but he didn't want to miss my visit. "Yessum, I've been tendin' it for 61 years."

Diaries written by women and men in these parts are fonts of knowledge that otherwise might have disappeared on subjects as diverse as farming, the first electric power lines, and local clothing factories.

Worley's Nursery
March 1993

Spring has come to Melvin Worley's out-kitchen.

There, on a table next to a kerosene stove, the 75-year-old is busy creating fruit trees. Bench grafting, it is called, a process whereby the scion or bud wood of a particular

variety—in this case, apple, pear or flowering crab trees—
is attached to individually selected rootstock to create a
custom-made fruit tree.

Melvin has been in the nursery business at Worley's
Nursery on Braggtown Road, York Springs, since he was
a child; his late father started it in 1913. Last December
Melvin suffered a stroke, but it hasn't held him back and
it won't keep spring away.

Right now he's busy bench grafting 200 saplings of different varieties to be sold at the Pennsylvania Association
of Conservation Districts' spring meeting in Wilkes-Barre.
As a past president of this organization, he recalls traveling extensively and is proud to donate his trees as a
fundraiser to help cover travel costs for others. In nearly
every county conservation district, spring brings such
seedling sales during which residents may buy a selection
of hardwoods and softwoods—everything from oaks and
maples to fir, spruce and pine trees, in addition to fruit
trees—for a nominal price. Proceeds fund conservation
measures of all kinds and environmental education pro-
grams for children in each of the counties.

Last weekend I visited Melvin, and while we talked, a
man stopped by with his children to place his order for
110 trees and an assortment of grape vines and berry
bushes. The orchard of a few peach, a few plum, nectarine,
sweet and sour cherry, pear, and apples of this and that
variety is for his young son, the man offered, and will support an eventual roadside market stand. "Oh yeah, and I
want a quince....My neighbor used to have 'em, and we'd
make jelly," he said, sitting at Melvin's kitchen table to
fill out his order form. His enthusiasm was infectious and
when he finished placing his order we all moved next door
to observe the grafting operation.

Known for his Old Timers, 50 or so old-time varieties
of apple trees, Melvin buds most of his stock in the field in

August, using the common propagation technique whereby a bud from the desired fruit tree is placed under the bark of a stem of root stock. But while successful budding is done in the early fall, grafting can be performed in the spring when buds of the scion wood are still dormant.

On this day the Cornell University graduate was grafting Smokehouse apple to M-VII semi-dwarfing rootstock. From a bucket of water, he took the rootstock, cut off the top at a sharp angle and made a downward cut with his knife through the center and just under the heartwood at the center. With the scion, he did the same, leaving two leaf buds. The stock and the scion were then slipped together so that their cambium layers—the area between the bark and the wood of the tree—locked in a hug.

"Watch and remember," the man told his son as Melvin wrapped the union with waxed string, clipped the redundant bud wood off the top, and dipped the cuts in a can of paraffin heating on the kerosene stove. The nurseryman explained that he started budding and grafting the old timers 25 years ago in order to bring back some of the varieties forgotten in today's pursuit of the perfect fruit. Now he and his son Chester offer an assortment that often need less spraying than the more widely cultivated commercial varieties.

"That's what I'm workin' on now if the good lord gives me enough time," he said. Some of their names are musical: Cox Orange Pippin, Duchess of Oldenburg, Henry Clay, King David, Lady Sweet, Meade Gravenstein, Molly Delicious, Old Virginia Winesap, Pound Sweet, Red Spy, Roxbury Russett, Salome, Permain, Wolf River, and Black Gilliflower, also called Sheepnose.

Shortly, Melvin, his son and their small staff will start digging these and dozens of other fruit and landscaping varieties. The nursery will again smell of fertile earth and green, growing leaves. And it will be time to plant trees.

Melvin Worley moved to the Brethren Home at Cross Keys in 2008. His fruit stand and nursery are closed.

Ace in Old Age
January 1996

I'm learning grace from my aged dog, Ace.

Ace is the lumbering black Labrador retriever mix who's been here for most of the significant times of my life. A big-footed pup my mate held in his hands when he brought him home, Ace arrived when our youngest was ten and he went through puberty at almost the same time as our older son. One of the gang, this dog tagged along when they camped out by the neighbor's pond. He was there, too, when dripping wet, they mooned another neighbor from the banks of that same pond.

Until the last two years, he broke the trail for our cross-country skiing treks and sauntered along on every walk we took. He proudly loped out ahead of the pack, hips swinging in a rhythmic gait, tail held high. It was those same hips, weak in retrievers, that eventually halted his walks.

Now he is 14—98 in human terms, though I suspect the average life span for dogs has risen along with that of their human masters. Old Graybeard, I call him now that his muzzle has gone almost completely white along with the sparse brows above his big brown eyes.

His heart is good, the vet reports. And what a heart he has in that deep, big chest. Never loud or overbearing, Ace errs only by loving to excess. Though he has grown hard of hearing, he senses when friends approach the house and drags himself from his cedar-chip bed to wait by the kitchen door. He wags in greeting with every part of his bulk and finds their dangling hands with his head. If they don't respond to his nudges with petting, he leans into them or sits on their feet.

No, nothing is wrong with Ace's heart. It's just his posterior that has become a problem. As we grow old, our muscles atrophy. It's the same for dogs, our vet informs us. Sometimes, when he's had an accident, Ace turns, looks hopelessly at his rear end and then back at us as if to say, "It's such a small part of me. There's really nothing wrong with my head."

Indeed, the animal who used to spend three-fourths of his time sleeping seems now to have realized he has little time left. He is, I think, an example of aging gracefully. He has sized up the situation and determined that there is no time for crankiness or surliness. When I come home at night, I find him sitting by the door, waiting for me. Though it takes great effort these days, he pulls his hulk up to greet me, smiling that woolly, big-hearted smile with faded eyes.

I suspected Ace's sight was failing when he started bumping into us. Now he feels his way, one paw at a time, when inching across unfamiliar territory. Yet he still looks dolefully at us, then at his dish, if we forget to feed him. His hearing, too, appears selective. While simple commands fall on deaf ears, he always hears the opening of the refrigerator compartment where bologna and cheese are kept.

It is in these, his golden years, that Ace has refined his sense of humor. Where once he might have felt neglected during Friday night pizza suppers, he now has perfected a famished look that is pure schstick. He can turn it off and on at the drop of a crust.

By sheer force of will, this near-centenarian canine drags himself up the stairs to our bedroom at night. Once he's on the second floor, it's the morning descent that gives him pause. He moves in stages, yawning and stretching in his now-abbreviated style. His ears perk up like a pup's before he struggles, first to a sitting position, and then to his feet. Sometimes, when he's sitting on the old planked pine floor, his front feet slowly slide apart and out from under him, and he looks around as if to say, "Wish these tightwads would spring for wall-to-wall carpeting." And he takes what must be that first terrifying step before careening down the steep farmhouse stairway like a dump truck with worn-out brakes.

Yes, Ace is a good role model for man or beast. Time and the wear and tear it brings may have taken his mobility, but age has refined and enriched his personality. He remains cheerful and animated in ways that were impossible in his youth. And his greatest pleasure is in giving more love and comfort than he gets.

That's what I call grace.

Ace is buried in the same sunny spot where he liked to snooze in our back yard.

Tax Lady
April 1998

It won't be the same, paying taxes in Huntington Township this year. Jeannette Stambaugh, tax collector for more than 30 years, has retired.

I'm not the first to wonder how a Democrat managed to stay in an elected office for that long in a south-central Pennsylvania community where the geography is rural, agricultural, and distinctly Republican.

"People always ask me that," Jeannette told me. "I was appointed the year Harrison Fair ran for county commissioner." When Harrison, also a Democrat, moved to the Adams County Courthouse, the judge appointed Jeannette to fill the remaining two years of his term; she was re-elected every four years thereafter until 1997, when she decided not to run.

If paying taxes is a distasteful affair in any geographic area, here in the place where my family and I relocated 23 years ago, it always seemed to help that we knew the person who was responsible for collecting them. When we wrote what seemed a breathtakingly large property tax check every year, it helped to imagine the friendly, flint-haired woman whose name and address we also wrote on the envelope. If we had a question, all we had to do was pick up the phone and call.

"Jeannette?" I ventured on just such a call this winter. I'd misplaced my tax records for the last year and needed to know the amount we'd paid before completing our federal income tax return.

"No, this is her sister," a less-familiar voice responded, explaining that Jeannette still did have the old records on file and still was responsible for last year's school taxes. However, Jeannette was at her daughter's house recovering from a recent surgery.

"Didn't you know?" she replied when I inquired about her sister's health. "Jeannette had to have her right leg amputated." I gasped. Five years ago, she'd lost her husband—now this. A circulation problem had diminished the blood supply to her leg. Within two weeks of learning about her condition and having an artery graft and unsuccessful first surgery below the knee, she'd nearly died. Her doctor performed emergency surgery on her at 8 o'clock at night, amputating the leg just below the hip to save the 76-year-old woman's life.

"Now about your records," her sister said. "Did you try calling the courthouse?" I had, knowing about Jeannette's retirement, I told her, but they referred me back to Huntington Township. "Well, we'll look them up and get back to you," Jeannette's sister offered warmly. And in less than an hour, she did.

A few months later, I went to visit with the woman who'd survived all those years of Republican-dominated politics. Looking just as bright as ever, Jeannette rolled her wheelchair out to her daughter's kitchen, and we talked about her career, her brief illness and her prosthesis.

"They've got me walking now with a four-footed cane," she said, extolling the virtues of physical therapy. "I can go stairs." It was difficult at first without the muscles she needed to help her lift her leg, the dignified, sliver-haired woman conceded. "It's unbelievable...your balance leaves you—you're lopsided. To learn [balance] over again isn't easy, but it's possible."

"It's just not going to be the same around here," I told her, changing the subject.

"I must tell you a funny one," Jeannette piped, offering the story of a woman who mistakenly came to her house this year to pay her taxes.

"I can't understand," the woman said. "I got a different tax notice this year. It's from an entirely strange tax collector." The woman had mailed the tax notice back to the new collector, saying that he certainly must be mistaken because her tax collector had "always been Jeannette."

Nowadays, everything is computerized at the county courthouse, but in the earlier part of Jeannette's career, the collector made out her own tax notices, figuring each property owner's tax based on the assessment. Now, she offered, there are many people whose taxes are paid automatically—and impersonally—through their mortgage companies. "They have no idea what their tax is or where it goes."

Perhaps it was the personal attention she gave to people that made them trust her for all those years, I suggested.

"I understand both sides," she admitted, "because we

used to scratch fiercely to get [our own] taxes paid...but they were always paid."

During her tenure, few properties in Huntington Township were ever sheriff-sold. On the occasions when she had to place a lien against a property, she always talked with the owner first, and he or she usually found a way to pay it off. When property owners came upon difficult times, she'd allow them to pay their taxes in installments based upon the amounts of their various separate taxes. And seldom was there a bad check.

She collected taxes at her kitchen table until her husband built a separate office for her in the house on Stillhouse Road. She collected taxes on Saturdays and Sundays, and she got out of bed when people wanted to pay their tax at the very last minute, at 11 o'clock at night on deadline days.

One man used to write on his check, "This tax paid under protest," she recalled with a smile. "I don't know why, because nobody ever saw it but me."

"I think the thing that I always tried to do was to help people. If they had a problem, I'd say, 'Well, let's not worry about it now. Things will probably work out.' And they usually did.

"I miss the people, but everything changes. This is my job now," she said, pointing to her new leg and smiling that same positive, dignified smile.

Yes, I thought, things will work out. Jeannette will survive this momentary inconvenience with the same spunk that enabled her to survive our political geography all these years. Still, it won't be the same paying taxes in Huntington Township this year.

Jeannette Stambaugh passed away in 2006. In the difficult economic times of 2009, taxpayers hereabouts would feel good to see her reassuring smile again.

Baird Hershey Turns 90
January 1999

Last Sunday, the pastor of Baird Hershey's church an-
nounced in front of the entire congregation at Morning
Hour Chapel near York Springs, "I want to congratulate
Baird on being 90 years old today....But there's something
I want to know: How do you get to be that way?"

"You start early," Baird replied.

He ought to know. Recently I walked through the natural history section of the Carnegie Museum in Pittsburgh, just as I had so many times in my childhood. This
time, I paid particular attention, knowing that our Adams
County naturalist had begun learning the art of taxidermy—often a necessary skill for early taxonomists, who
at that time were still busy collecting and classifying new
animal species—when he was an 11-year-old living in Al-
legheny County. When you get to age 90, you have a lot of
stories to tell, and this story was one of the first Baird told
to me and others who call him friend.

The museum was his favorite hangout, for he was
most interested in the groupings of mammals. Museum
workmen, mostly artisan immigrants from Europe or
Asia, saw the boy hanging around so much, especially on
Saturdays, that they asked him if he'd like to help. And
before long, young Baird was working weekends at the
Carnegie for 50 cents an hour.

Eventually, the head man, Remi Santens from Italy,
noticed Baird admiring his work. If Baird would like to
learn taxidermy, Santens offered, all he need do was bring
in a dead pigeon or a crow and Santens would teach him.
Later, the youngster began working on a barred owl and
finished it one evening when Santens was working late,
sculpting a rhinoceros from plaster.

Baird looked out the window to see the moon rising

114

and knew his mother would be worried about his being so late, but he had to bide his time for just the right moment to present his question. Why, he asked Santens, was his owl, which he had mounted on a T-perch, slowly falling forward? Santens picked up the bird and felt the legs.

"Here's the problem," he told the boy, "you're missing the second joint." Baird stayed at the museum that night, working until the owl stood tall.

Lots of Baird's friends know about the owl that wouldn't stand up straight. Stories such as this were exchanged by more than 300 of the Hersheys' friends and family who gathered in the social room of the York Springs Fire Hall Sunday to celebrate with him and his wife, Laura.

It seemed fitting that one of Baird's sons-in-law would connect owls with courting his wife. Larry Schweiger, now executive director of the Western Pennsylvania Conservancy, remembers seeing a great-horned owl in the Hersheys' woods on his first date with Baird's youngest daughter, Clara.

"It's not many men who can claim that their father-in-law introduced them to their wife," said the younger man. Yet when Larry asked Baird for Clara's hand, the older man told him: "I need to set up a meeting with you....I love Clara very much and I want to make sure she's making a good choice." Baird finally accepted his proposal and became a surrogate father for Larry when his own father died just after the wedding.

Baird's son, his daughters, grandchildren, other family members and dozens of friends were invited by Laura to commemorate the occasion. Among their remembrances were:

- Baird's 16 gardens of azaleas, rhododendrons and fruit trees;
- the hundreds of people who've knocked on the Hersheys' door wanting the well-known naturalist to

identify a tree, a snake or a wildflower or tell them why their plant was sick;

- his vegetable gardens that provided "lots of turnips, potatoes and cabbage" for his family during the Great Depression;
- his fall through the barn roof when he was 80;
- the time after eye surgery when he drove his tractor into the lake;
- the tire he blew on the pickup truck while hauling his own granite tombstone home from Vermont;
- and the 400 copies of Billy Graham's book, *A Closer Walk with Thee*, that Baird has given away.

The day before the party, he measured the thickness of the ice on the lake at Hershey's Fur Center Campground, which the couple has operated on their grounds for decades. "Baird has known for a long while that the climate is becoming warmer," his son-in-law said, because every winter for four generations a Hershey has measured the ice on the lake and recorded its thickness.

At the end of the party, family, neighbors, members of the Audubon Society, Hershey's Fur Center summer campers, Rhododendron Society folks, farmers, conservationists and gardeners all sang his favorite song to the new nonagenarian: "You are my sunshine..." And we all were glad that our friend had started early.

I came to know Baird and Laura when we started taking our sheepskins to Hershey's Fur Center for tanning. I used to love wandering into the workroom where Laura sewed deerskins into soft, sweet-smelling leather coats. At an annual meeting of the local Audubon Society, I, too, saw the great-horned owls and learned to identify these huge birds' twiggy nests in the Hersheys' woods. Baird died in 2001, but his legacy is in good hands. Laura still runs the campground and sends out an annual family Christmas letter detailing the accomplishments of their many offspring, including the announcement a few years back that their son-in-law, quoted above, had become executive director of the National Wildlife Federation in Washington, D.C.

The Graham house as it looked not long after John Guise, second from left, built it, circa 1890, adding to an older structure at the rear.

Lisle, Kirk (holding Ace), Eileen and John Graham pose in front of the solar addition to their house, 1984.

John pauses while reconstructing an ironstone fence near the old chicken coop in the back yard.

Parsley stayed inside the pasture fence on this day.

Eileen and Lisle, ready for corn planting.

Guise's Cash Store owner, Gertie Guise, holds Nellie Guise Riley's brothers, Gilbert and Robert, in 1919 or 1920.

Johnnie Everhart could have been muskrat or raccoon trapper of the year in this 1940 photo. He was named to the Pennsylvania Trappers Association's Hall of Fame in 2007.

Baird Hershey feeding his chickadee friend. "It would come each day for its sunflower seeds, and if I was caught without any seed in my pocket, it would dart at my head, chirping loudly," he wrote on the back of this picture.

Hazel Johnson, in her nineties, looks over a tree her nephews have cut down in her yard. In the summer, this tree was home to a large black snake.

Edith Kline Bupp and Paul Bupp, Sr., posed for this picture in the early 1980s.

Bunny leans over the barnyard gate on a misty day.

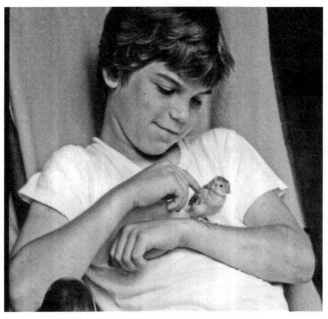

Kirk and Cheep Cheep enjoy a quiet moment.

Eileen shows off Spunky and her triplets.

Melvin Worley proudly sported his apple hat while tending
his fruit stand.

Worley's Nursery as it appeared in the 1930s. The car in the foreground advertised races at nearby Latimore Fairgrounds.

Charlotte and Wilbur were George's successors.

CR

Harold C. "Bud" Miller built bluebird houses and other things in his basement workshop.

Howard and Mary Starner at a birthday party, for which Irene undoubtedly baked the cake.

127

Hickory Point School picture, 1939-40. Front Row: Lloyd Spertzel, Fred Emlet, Richard Keckler, Bob Spertzel, Stanley Bupp, Jim Hicks. Middle row: Lucille Bupp, Joan Miller, Jack Asper, Bill Riley, Richard Spertzel, Kenneth Bupp, Paul Bupp, Jr. Back row: Elwood Thumma, Arlene Miller, Blanche Sowers, Grace Spangler (teacher), Miriam Emlet, Vena Jean Nell, Dick Wilman.

Twirly Top as it appeared in 2009.

Chapter 4
Garnets and Diamonds in the Rough
CR

It's hard for mere mortals to judge anything on its surface. We'd come to Adams County because we wanted acreage and it was one of the last undeveloped places, a place where we could afford to buy land. Still, everything has its price. If I wanted the bucolic life—farm *and* career—someone had to pay for it either with elbow grease or by sacrificing one thing to get another. For a while, it seemed my life would be dominated by hard work and rough, uphill climbs. Often, I failed to see the depth of character and simple beauty that were right in front of me. Then I began to understand that writing about these experiences—looking at the broader perspective when words are committed to paper—allowed me to laugh rather than cry. I shared my innermost joys and disappointments with readers and found that, even in these rocky hills, I was no longer a community of one.

Red Raspberries in the Rain
November 1985

Money may buy a ticket to Monte Carlo or a spot on the beach at Aruba this winter, but it can't buy red raspberries in the rain.

It rained again that day, despite the weatherman's prediction for clearing, sunny weather. The kids were safely on the school bus, the house was empty. I needed a hot shower this cold autumn morning just to get my bones moving. Another winter approached. In a few short months, another year would end, and I had yet to catch up with forty-two summers all too casually spent.

The rain came down in a slow, steady curtain, but it seemed a sacrilege to wish it away in this, a drought year, when moisture must be regained before the ground hardened with winter frost. So I lingered through the morning television shows before putting on the stiff, vinyl raincoat and crusty rubber boots to do my chores.

It had been a frustrating year. My horse had come up lame, healed, and got sick all over again. I'd recovered from an accident, emerged from a cast ready to tackle the world, and discovered I had less to tackle it with. My husband had to have knee surgery in the middle of a remodeling project that was yet to be finished. We took walks and commiserated: this must be how it feels to grow old.

I fed the steers, mushing through the rain-soaked feedlot. I mucked the horse's shed, scraped some of the mud from her thickening winter coat and took her temperature. If she didn't perk up soon, we'd have to call the vet.

Then came the sheep, the goat, the cats and dog. When everyone was fed, I could go to the cellar to do laundry and pick lint off all the Orlon socks waiting in the dryer. Soon rain would wash these brightly colored autumn leaves away and the sky would assume the color of lint.

It was another dreary day. Upstairs languished a word processor with an empty gray screen. A book was waiting, waiting to be written. Like the old pickup truck when I needed a bale of hay, it hadn't yet got started. We were both experiencing ignition problems—stalled in these agonizing, interminable moments. As I rounded the bend past the hedgerow that every year seemed to grow more tangled with wild honeysuckle, I thought how it would be to miss the heady smell of summer, this winter more than ever.

Beyond the house, the garden looked barren except for some leftover chard and bug-eaten broccoli. Tomatoes that should have brought us the ripe warmth of summer now would be supplanted with produce-counter imitations. They bloomed too late and never really did get started. Adjacent were our berry bushes, dripping rivers from silver-green leaves that clung to the drooping purple canes. They'd produced a crop in summer and were dying back.

"Time to prune," I thought, until I saw them. Red, faceted gems—raspberries growing miraculously in the rain. Sometimes there was a second crop, early in September if we were lucky. But raspberries now in the late days of October were unheard of. I ran to the house for a bucket.

They were soft and wet—garnets dripping with diamonds, exotic as passion fruit and hand-picked coconuts. They were the sun-drenched French Riviera, Acapulco and Hawaii. Some fell apart in my fingers, others made it whole into the bucket, still others melted to a raspberry rain in my mouth.

I took them in the house and poured profusely into the requisite morning bowl of bran. The purist would have said they were unclean; I saw no need to wash them. Tiny insects crawled up the sides of the cereal bowl as the milk flowed in, and now and then a moldy berry floated to the top. I removed my fogged bifocals and ate hungrily.

Yes, winter is coming. The rain will turn to ice and snow, just as the old pickup will refuse to start. But I will remember raspberries in the October rain and the taste of endless summer.

More than 20 years later, I continue to keep red raspberry bushes and consider their fruit the ultimate breakfast luxury.

The Sweep's Hat is Always Black
November 1986

FOR SALE: Used wood stove in good working order. Comes with slightly soiled chimney sweep, two dead birds and a dehydrated bat. Cheap.

It was a sunny Indian summer Saturday. The house was clean, the windows sparkled. In honor of the approaching Thanksgiving holiday, I had starched and ironed the kitchen curtains. Everything was going well until a voice called from the cellar: "It's time to clean the chim-ney."

"What?"

"You know," said the voice, now in the kitchen, arms laden with rods and brushes. "It happens every year. We have to clean the chimney."

The chimney he referred to belongs to a big double-door wood stove in my kitchen, the same wood stove I had closed up last spring and ignored all summer. It is an ugly, stained cast iron master that eats logs and manufactures dirt. When oil prices came down last summer, I had the tank in the cellar filled on the qt. And when the warm autumn days fell off, I fell on the thermostat. This year, I thought we might forget about the wood stove.

"You know we have to clean the chimney before we start up the fire," hummed the voice.

Let me explain that when most of his contemporaries were frolicking in a little upstate New York village named Woodstock my husband and others, inspired by predictions of the Arab oil embargo, rallied at a place called Woodstove in the Pennsylvania highlands.

No, the wood stove wasn't my idea. But it was supposed to save us money *after* he paid off the chain saw and a heavy-duty pickup truck. It promised a return to the good old days when people were self-sufficient, when a Saturday outing meant a day chopping wood in the fresh air, and when a family ritual was the annual chimney cleaning.

After the first year of chopping, stacking, chasing bugs around my kitchen, dusting, sweeping, and treating poison ivy, I was ready for a return—to the good old days of central heating. When we were carelessly dependent on oil barons, when a family outing meant a ski trip, and when the energy people most wanted to conserve was their own.

Such was not my lot. In fact, the only lot I saw thereafter was a wood lot. Adding insult to injury, once a year my husband became a grinning, demonic chimney sweep. "Some enchanted evening, you may meet a stranger..." sang the sweep as he dismantled the stovepipe and screwed together his rods and brushes.

"Why do you s'pose they paint these things black," he chuckled. Family ritual, nothing. Everyone else in the family—kids, cats, even the black dog—disappeared on chimney-cleaning day.

"Don't you think it's time we got rid of this thing?" I sighed as the singing sweep handed me a flashlight and a plastic garbage bag. As usual, I was left holding the bag on these occasions.

"Oh no! Why, what would we gather 'round on a cold winter's eve if we had no fire?"

"How about an electric space heater?"

"C'mon now. Have you ever heard of chestnuts roasting on an open space heater?" I mentioned that nobody in our family likes chestnuts. But the sweep shoved a wire porcupine brush and three stories' worth of extension rods into the chimney, instructing me to shine the light up into the flue.

"See that? Why, it's hardly even dirty in there," he

chortled. And, with a whoosh and the tinkling of tiny black particles bounding down the metal pipe, I was covered with soot, head to foot.

"Uh-oh," said the sweep. "You forgot to hold the bag."

"Bag, my eye," I yelled. "This thing is a menace."

"Something in your eye?" he cooed.

"It's a filthy menace!" I sputtered, broom in hand. "Birds and things get caught in here and can't get out."

"Naw...Say, don't you think I oughta' have a top hat?"

While I showered, he reconnected the pipe, moved the stove back in place and brought in an armload of wood. The kids, the cats and the black dog resumed their appropriate positions around the hearth, and we opened the stove doors to light the season's first fire.

"Gross!" yelled the kids; the black dog skulked away.

There on the ash-covered grate were a wizened wren, a stiff starling, five June bugs, legs up, and a dehydrated bat.

"Bring on the kindling," called the sweep. "Next year, I'm gonna wear a hat."

The very same Timberline wood burning stove we bought during the Carter Administration heats our house yet today, providing us year-round exercise, gathering, cutting and splitting logs to feed its crackling winter fires.

Plum Puddings
October 1986

What could be better? We've had our first snowfall of the season, and I am going home with one of Gladys Shearer's plum puddings.

Gladys is my egg lady. She's grown hard of hearing in recent years and her brow is knotted in a dark squint because she doesn't see well anymore. She isn't the inviting kind of person you'd pick out on the street to talk to, but Gladys has the Christmas spirit and it's cooked into her plum pudding.

I like going to Gladys's house. The lane winds down a steep hill and across a pond full of ducks and geese. I have to stop halfway up the other side and wait for assorted chickens to cross the road; one ancient guinea cock hobbles along behind. In summer a mother and her yellow ducklings waddle through the grass. In winter a kettle bubbles on the wood-burning stove in Gladys's sitting room. From the living room a grandfather clock chimes the hour at least once while I'm there—nobody just dashes in and out of Gladys's to pick up a dozen eggs.

From November through December the aroma of steaming cinnamon, mace, cloves and oranges fills her house. "Wouldn't be Christmas without plum pudding," she says.

Traditional English Christmas pudding apparently started during the Elizabethan period, according to Lorna Sass, author of *Christmas Feasts from History,* published by Irene Chalmers Cookbooks, Inc., New York, 1981. It suffered a temporary Puritanical banishment along with merrymaking during the 17th century and flourished during Queen Victoria's reign.

Gladys's plum pudding tradition started when she married some 39 years ago and was requested by her husband, Herb, to make "a pudding like mom used to." It took some time but eventually she came upon an agreeable recipe in an old Pennsylvania Dutch cookbook. To it she added a bit of variation. Now she cooks several hundred of these traditional desserts a season without looking at the recipe, transforming her farmhouse into a pudding factory. Still, they are not whipped up en masse—each pudding is made separately.

For Gladys the season starts in October when nuts

begin dropping from hickory and black walnut trees on her farm. "You have to get them in October to beat the squirrels," she says. Even earlier she begins drying orange peels and fruits. For the family, she makes a special pudding with apples, apricots, peaches or pears dried on the wood stove in the previous season.

Suet, an essential part of traditional plum pudding, sometimes presents a problem. Though beef suet will do most of the time, some of her customers whose families originated in the Far East request sheep or goat suet for cultural reasons. Gladys trims the meat scraps from the fat and chops it into small pieces.

On this day she has assembled all the ingredients on a tray for me to see: 1 cup suet, chopped fine; 1 cup sugar; 2 cups coarse bread crumbs; 1 cup flour; 2 eggs, slightly beaten; 1 cup milk; 1/4 cup fruit juice (today it is pear juice); several pinches dried orange peel; 1 teaspoon cloves; 2 teaspoons cinnamon; 1 teaspoon mace; ½ teaspoon salt; 1 teaspoon baking soda; 2 cups raisins; a generous ½ cup nutmeats; and ½ cup mixed candied fruit.

"It says 'currants,'" Gladys notes of the original recipe, which calls for a cup each of currants and raisins, "but currants is nothin' but a small grape, you know, so I use raisins because currants are so hard to get."

She mixes the first three ingredients in her electric mixer on low. Next, the juice, orange rind and eggs are added; the flour is sifted and blended with the spices, and a small amount of this is used to coat the fruits and nuts "so they don't stick together in the pudding," she instructs me. Then she adds the milk and flour mixtures alternately, slowly pouring each in the mixing bowl. Finally the pudding is poured into an old tin mold, the lid secured, and placed to steam for three hours in a kettle of bubbling water on the wood stove.

In Victorian England, Christmas pudding began on

"Stir-Up Sunday" five weeks before Christmas. Named for the first line of the church Collect for that day, which beseeched the Lord to "stir up" the faithful, according to Sass, who says it was considered good luck for each member of the family to stir the pudding before cooking began.

Now there is only one person to stir at Gladys's house. After a long illness, Herb passed away last year near Thanksgiving. Some of us worried about Gladys then. They'd had no children and for years she had cared for her husband alone. Once an Army Corps of Engineers employee and world traveler, Herb became bedfast with emphysema. Lately he'd been dependent on a respirator and was totally dependent on his wife, who dared not leave the house except for a few hours when the visiting nurse came by. At the end, Gladys was hard-pressed even to get out for the mail or to feed the chickens. How would she survive now, suddenly free and utterly alone?

She called me for help with writing the obituary. Weeks later, the grandfather clock was chiming when I stopped in for eggs. The house smelled of cloves and cinnamon, and on the stove two puddings sat, steaming. Gladys bustled in the kitchen.

"Got all these orders from the country club.... Just wouldn't be Christmas without plum pudding."

Gladys and Herb loved history and found on their place stone artifacts that may have dated back to Native Americans who inhabited their farmland in prehistoric times.

Ode to an Old Goat
March 1987

It's a rite of spring that finds me waiting in this old barn for lambs to be born. While others frolic on Florida beaches, I sit here on hay bales, chaff scratching my neck. Overhead, a March wind sends cobwebs dancing among the rough old timbers; down below, the cold stings my fingers, toes and dripping nose.

But this year, the lambs were late. This spring I sat in the barn waiting for an old goat to die.

Pansy—she had sisters named Daisy and Petunia—is a grade Nubian, white with floppy ears, a goatee and wattles dangling from her chin. We brought her home in the back of an old Ford Station wagon when she was just a few weeks old; the first farm animal we acquired, she made us legitimate country dwellers. It was obvious from the beginning, however, that Pansy would be a pet, not just a piece of livestock. As the one ordained to feed her four times daily with a baby bottle, I established a bond with this goat and she took it seriously, showing up at my kitchen door when she apparently figured it was time for tea.

I learned from her that the myths about goats are untrue. For one thing, she didn't smell bad. Although males become pruriently pungent during mating season, females are fastidiously clean and ladylike in their behavior. And she didn't eat tin cans. However, typical of goats, she had a taste for wiry, bushy scrub growth. We didn't get Pansy for her milk, which would have acquired a peculiar taste from the weeds and brush she ate, so we set her to work clearing thickets of wild raspberries and burdock that had overgrown our place. And poison ivy. She relished poison ivy. In the cleared spaces we planted pine trees, azaleas and grape vines—and she relished these, too.

On numerous occasions we tried to have our nanny goat bred. Each time it was the same. Come fall, we'd tell her she was going on a picnic and hop her into the back of the same old station wagon. A half-mile down the road, she'd be in the back seat. Another quarter-mile, she'd climbed to the front. And by the mile mark, I was driving with a full-grown goat wrapped around my neck. I'm sure it made interesting conversation for the people in cars going in the opposite direction: two heads in the driver's seat, one of them definitely not a cocker spaniel, would be enough to get anybody's goat.

Most times the picnic results were less than we expected—cute as she was, Pansy was no Shirley Jones and the lecherous neighborhood billy was no William Holden. However, one time the fall frolicking did produce the desired effect and Pansy became the mother of two feisty brown and white kids named Truman and Roosevelt, who scaled fences, stone walls and car fenders with dexterity and provided us with numerous New Deal-style public works projects.

Without a doubt, Pansy was queen of the barnyard. When we got young sheep, she took over as their mother. She butted dogs, calves and boys out of her royal realm. Even the ram was intimidated by her style. But in the years that passed, nearly 13 by now, she never forgot her affection for me.

No one could have told me that a goat would be cuddly till I held her as a baby. Even now, when she is off her feed, a pat on the head and a scratch on the chin seems to nourish her. Her decline had started a few summers back when we returned from vacation to find she'd suffered some kind of episode. A mild heart attack, a small stroke—we were never sure—had slowed her down. But a few weeks later she rallied and came back, ornery as ever. Then, too, there was the arthritis. On really cold mornings, she needed help getting up for breakfast. In fact, it was the cold that seemed to undo her when winter returned with typical vengeance after a brief warm spell in early spring. She lost her appetite and seemed to lose her cud. (Like other ruminants, goats constantly chew their cud as part of the digestive process.) We took to feeding her leaf lettuce from the table and apples or anything that would hold her interest. I petted her and told her that soon the grass would grow and lambs would come. That she'd make it for another year if she could just hang on for now. But she ate less and less. Each morning when I un-latched the barn door to let the sun shine in, I prepared for the worst. One night I looked up the knacker's phone number.

I sat in the barn, flexing my own stiff hands and feet, thinking how unkind spring is, promising us jonquils when all the while we feel like flies just crawling out of the woodwork.

A robin sang. I'd seen lots of birds so far this season, but this was the first robin's song I'd heard. Then the dog barked and Pansy hobbled to her feet. She nosed her feed dish and started eating. Later, when I checked on her, she was standing in the barnyard, looking again for all the world like a crotchety queen. Once again, Pansy is wait-ing for lambs to be born—any day now. It's a rite of spring.

In our first or second spring on the farm, our boys submitted Pansy as their entry in the elementary school's pet show. She didn't win first place, but she was very popular among the students and parents.

Cross-Country Ski
January 1988

Into the quiet of new snow we step. The sky is electric black with a charge of mauve in the direction of far-off towns as we head cross country on the skinny skis.

Nordic skiing, it's called. But we've never been to Scandinavia. It's what we wait for every year when snow time comes: two of us and a black dog setting out the back door across last year's hay and next year's wheat on narrow boards that schuss and slide in Pennsylvania farm powder.

The skis and boots are secondhand. And the haute couture of our slopes consists of long warm socks, a pair of jeans without holes, a barn jacket, hat and gloves. It doesn't pay to overdress. You exercise a lot of muscles with cross-country skiing, and too many clothes can make you too hot. Then again, in farm country there's nobody to impress. Especially with night skiing.

At night this time of year there are no noises for the eyes or ears. No snowplows or snowmobiles, no deer hunters or deer spotters. Nothing to break the white silence but the hoo-hoo-hoos from an owl in the hollow. It is so quiet you can hear snow and ice and pine breathing.

Where we go are no groomed trails. Though in deep snow we appreciate snowmobiles that have preceded us and packed a path, tonight we make our way across winter-fallow fields bedded with corn stubble and rocks that scratch their marks on the laminated ski bottoms. Stems of wild aster and goldenrod bend easily under the white cushion where we kick and glide. Brittle skeletons of Queen Anne's lace snap as we break over the flat. Barbed multiflora rose fingers snatch at our pants and socks.

Underfoot, a field mouse has been roused from his winter's nap; the black dog teases him for a while then returns to the trail, acknowledging that a sleepy mouse is not fair game.

Downhill runs are breath grabbers. Knees flexed, we launch from the crest of a neighbor's hill, skis humming, bodies pitched between flight and a runaway truck, elbows in, poles tucked. Downhilling on Nordic skis after dark is a risky business, but we know this run and the long stretch of soft grass that slows us at the bottom.

Uphill treks are not as easy for me at night. My partner plows full-speed ahead up a grade that seems much steeper than I remember while I slide back three steps for every one I take forward. I try the duck-foot herringbone and fall on my face. Sidestepping—first one ski then the other, one pole then the other, like a baby learning to climb stairs—is my only way to the top.

I am too slow, he calls. The dog doubles back to find me.

From up here we see lights, the yellow eyes of towns and houses, in every direction. We stop to watch and feel and listen before heading home.

Tomorrow we'll glide down Blue Berry Lane on these narrow boards to the woods back of the hollow. We'll bump down the steep path past the fat oak with snow glued to its windward side, sidestepping across fallen logs, ducking tree limbs. We'll slide across the frozen creek and trust the rippled ice. Then we'll pole to the top of Church Hill and stand under the tall pines to hear them sigh, and watch for the red-tailed hawk that soars in these back-woods fields. There will be jays and squirrels, a rabbit and perhaps a deer or fox if the black dog is quiet.

And there will be the schuss and the glide, the hum and the whistle.

The snow will turn phosphorescent blue at twilight as the sun sets in waves of flamingo pink and purple. We'll ski home and turn on the television to commercials for vacations in sunny Florida. And the next day we'll ski again.

In the early 1980s, our young friends, Paul and Linda Ebright, took us cross-country skiing, giving us a new perspective and a sport we could enjoy with little cost or fuss, for the rest of our lives.

Cleopatra Goose
July 1989

Would the person who dropped off a goose in front of my house please come forward? ...Be careful where you walk.

It's not unusual for abandoned puppies and kittens to appear on our doorstep, but never before did we find a fowl. It was about a week ago that my husband and one of our sons heard a ruckus and walked down to the intersection in front of the house to investigate. They returned with a goose trailing behind.

My husband laughed. "A rabid goose! It charged up to us so fast, honking and squawking, I thought it would start foaming at the mouth."

"It's somebody's pet," the boy, who adopted an orphaned pheasant chick when he was 10, beamed.

I telephoned neighbors to no avail. Those who keep geese had no missing members of their flocks. Those who have no geese thought it the funniest thing they'd heard: a foundling goose.

"You'll have to call the Pennsylvania Game Commission. We only take dogs and cats," offered a receptionist at the local animal shelter.

"Ma'am, we don't handle domestic animals," said an officer of the game commission. It was his advice to capture the goose, put it in a burlap sack and transport it to a pond or lake where there were other geese—sort of drop it off again.

"We can't do that, Ma," protested our son. "Look how nice she is."

Indeed, the goose seems to have made herself at home, staking out a territory next to the hulk of a 1969 Chevelle long ago retired to a spot behind the pig shed. Since geese like to eat insects, we figured she chose this locale because the old car, like most other stationary outdoor objects this time of year, is rife with the ubiquitous earwig, inch-long insects we call pincher bugs because of the pincer-like appendages near their heads.

And she does seem rather nice, smaller than the Toulouse geese a friend of ours keeps and, unlike the several ganders we've known before, not at all aggressive. It is too soon to tell because this goose is still quite young, but she seems to have the gentler personality of a female, our friend has advised. (Apparently, sexing geese is just as difficult as sexing chickens.) With its knobbed black beak and small body, ours is probably an Egyptian goose, she said, inquiring, "What are you going to call her?"

We thought Cleopatra would be a fitting name, owing to her breeding. And so the foundling goose has become Cleo.

Our friend has shown us how to catch a goose, walking up behind and grabbing the neck with one hand, body with another, carefully holding the posterior to one side. Ours is not unwilling to be caught. Once in our arms, she sits quietly—soft and warm, like a live down pillow—her head resting against her breast, doubled back on the silky S-curve of her long tan and brown neck.

Cleo is an altogether pleasant creature, with one exception: goose dung. Though she's declared her own territory, she ranges the entire back yard, leaving mounds of soupy green droppings at inconvenient places on our new brick walk.

"We'll keep her in the goat pasture," my husband determined, depositing the goose on the other side of a woven wire fence. She was inside the fence only momentarily. Since all the books advise that domestic geese can't fly, he surmised Cleo was crawling through the gate.

"She can stay with the sheep," he next declared, transporting the goose to her new digs. However, the sheep pen didn't suit her. Within minutes of her appearance, our two rams lumbered over to investigate this web-footed fowl. First the older, a big merino, nosed her, and she promptly pecked him on the head. Then, the younger, a small black sheep, stomped at her and assumed a charging position, to which the goose took serious offense, flapping her wings and flogging him in a fury. We walked away, pleased that Cleo was confined and could hold her own with the new neighbors. But in less than a half-hour, she was free again.

"Yuk! Why doesn't somebody teach this goose some manners?" moaned our younger son. He'd ventured outdoors barefoot.

Not the goose's fault said our friend when we complained. Goose dung is nothing more than digested grass clippings. A goose has no sphincter muscles, she explained, nature's way of keeping them empty and light, so they can fly.

"How soon is Thanksgiving?" my husband laughingly demanded.

Every barn cat we ever had—duly caught and taken to the vet for inoculations, worming, and neutering—was dumped in the country by a human who felt no compunction about abandoning it. A drop-off goose was something else altogether. We never had another goose after Cleo, who lived with us to a ripe old age.

Snake Doctor
May 1989

Gene Grove is a craggy-faced man—the kind who wears cowboy boots and talks in a drawl that's half country, half Baltimore. Both his arms bear multiple tattoos. He is not your typical herpetologist.

"Snake Doctor," reads the sign outside Grove's place. A friend made it for him, he says; on one side a cobra is painted, on the other is a Southeast Asian snake called a *krait*. During his off-hours, Grove, a demolition worker, runs an ongoing yard sale at a building that was once a restaurant and later a motorcycle shop along U.S. Route 30 west of Gettysburg. He rescues things most people don't want: used tires, clothing, motorcycle parts. And snakes. Grove has a reputation hereabouts as the man to call when people find a snake in their house and want someone to relocate it to its natural habitat.

"I've spent the best part of my life foolin' with 'em," he says. "My parents told me, when I was a little kid that the first thing I ever come home with was a baby copperhead." He earned his "doctor" designation by taking care of sick snakes that people bring to him.

Snakes get all kinds of diseases, according to Grove—fungal infections, mouth rot and mites, to name a few—and their mortality rate is high. In this part of Pennsylvania, poisonous snakes generally have one litter of young per year, with eight to 10 per litter. Of these, he observes, only one or two survive. Their worst enemy is man.

"If the birds don't get 'em, man will. They don't get a chance to really grow up … there's roads everywhere." He is out to convert those who think the only good snake is a dead snake. "It's the most misunderstood thing there is. The snakes we have around here [copperheads and timber rattlers] are not aggressive. They try to get away from you whenever they can. It's very rare that anyone is bit just walkin' around the mountain."

A self-taught naturalist, Grove claims he knows every snake den on South Mountain, the area of south-central Pennsylvania that covers Adams, Cumberland and Franklin counties and marks the northern end of the Blue Ridge Province of the Appalachians. Outcroppings of rock that are exposed to the sun most of the day indicate the den locations. It takes a week to 10 days of continuous warmth for snakes to move to the surface in late spring, he instructs, then they shed their skins and begin looking for food after their long hibernation. Drought brings them out of the mountains, looking for water. But when the temperature soars the way it did last summer, "you can't hardly find a snake" because it gets too hot for them, he tells me.

I have come to see Grove on a rainy spring day. As we sit discussing color phases, I am a little antsy among his collection of baby copperheads and timber rattlers lolling in a dry aquarium. His décor consists of snake skins, snake eggs in formaldehyde, snake fangs, and a freeze-dried Burmese python. Snakes suffer greatly from man's fears, Grove reminds me.

A first-rate superstition is the perennial story about black snakes and copperheads interbreeding. "That's folklore," he laughs, explaining that their breeding habits are entirely different: copperheads have live births; black snakes hatch from eggs.

In a room that once served as cold storage for the former restaurant, he shows me two beautifully marked timber rattlers about four feet long and an iridescent-skinned six-foot long black snake—all sleepily hibernating.

"The truth is, you've got to be secretive about where you find 'em," he says, because people have set the mountain on fire, trying to burn out the dens. If all the snakes were killed, Grove warns, rodents would overrun the country. "When we start foolin' around with the balance of nature, we mess things up pretty good."

Still, Grove doesn't recommend that novices go looking for snakes. He blames overconfidence for the close calls he's suffered. His right index finger was lost to a snake bite, and the eerily reptile-textured scar on his right arm bears testimony to a skin graft necessitated by a terrible snake-bite infection.

Why does he keep going back after such painful experiences? Snakes are "interesting...different all the time," he muses. "And I see things out in the forest that you only ever see once in a lifetime. A grouse hatchin' out her eggs and baby hawks hatchin'.... Things like that are hard to come by."

Gene Grove died in the 1990s—if memory serves me correctly—of complications resulting from snakebite. A furniture maker briefly occupied his former space along Route 30.

Runaway Bull
June 1990

Butter wouldn't melt in his mouth. With big black eyes and a wet black nose, he was the cutest little Holstein bull calf I'd ever seen, and he was tied to a tree next to my corncrib.

"What's up?" I asked a neighbor boy who was sitting across the road in his grandfather's pickup, standing guard it seemed. Out of the truck, he sprang, launching excitedly into a report about a raging bull that had led most of the neighborhood on a merry chase for the better part of the afternoon.

"He's a wild one, he is," pronounced the boy. He didn't know whom the bull calf belonged to but said half the population of York Springs, a good three miles away by road, had seen him barreling around the town.

A few days later, the same boy reported that with much ado the animal had been returned to its rightful owner, a small-time farmer who lives nine miles north in the direction of Dillsburg. "We grabbed him around the collar and backed him up against your hay elevator, and he just jumped and kicked and hollered somethin' awful," said the boy's uncle, Stan Bupp. Stan and four other members of his family finally got the animal loaded in their truck after Stan put his fingers in the calf's nose and led him to the pickup bed. This bit of husbandry is quite effective and recalls the practical purpose behind the traditional ring in a bull's nose. Stan's brother, June (short for Junior), had performed a similarly impressive move for us not long after we moved to the farm by leading our angry hog onto a trailer by his ears and tail.

After they tied him in the pickup bed, the freedom-loving bovine threw himself on the floor and kicked and bawled for all he was worth, according to Stan. "He cut every caper there was to cut," he laughed. "Put a big dent in June's tailgate." After phoning everyone in the area they could think of who might have lost an animal, Stan said they called the Pennsylvania State Police.

"'I caught about a 400-pound bull here yesterday morning,' I told the officer. He started laughin' and said a lady just called in and said she'd lost one...When they got here, I noticed her husband didn't have rails on the sides of his truck. That little bull had 'em beat all apart,"

Brenda and John Holder and their teenage daughters live in the next county and dabble in farming with a few goats, a few sheep and sundry other animals on a small farm similar to the part-time operation we also had. They'd bought the calf at a livestock market the night before, Brenda told me when I called her later. They hadn't even got him out of the stockyard till he ran away. "And once he got a taste of freedom, we couldn't get him tied again," she said. They'd loaded him in the pickup bed, but he leapt out, right over its side rails.

In the parking lot, "He put a dent in some man's truck, and we have to pay for it," she recalled good-naturedly. With Brenda driving and her husband holding on to the calf in back, they rumbled out of the stock market gates.

"We got about a mile down the road, and I could feel the truck pitching. I pulled over and said, 'John, are you all right?' 'No,' he said. He wrestled that calf the whole way home. About 45 minutes." Finally they got their new bull calf home and bedded down.

"My husband named him Buddy," Brenda said. "All the way home, he kept talking in his ear, trying to get close to him." The next morning they fed the calf and left the house for work at about 6:30 a.m. Brenda laughed, noting that one of her neighbors spied him a mile down the road at quarter till seven.

All that night, the Holders searched for Buddy to no avail. The next morning, John stopped two women out for a walk and asked if they'd seen a bull on the loose.

"Oh my, yes. And that bull was moving," one of them said. "He had froth in his mouth!" People all down Mountain Road had seen him. One woman was feeding her dog and said to her hired hand, "George, come catch this bull." The man was gone for a while and came back into the yard, wheezing and shaking his head. "Nope," he said, "that bull's too fast for me."

Brenda traced her bull calf to York Springs, where he'd apparently stopped by the feed mill to slurp up some corn that had fallen to the ground, and to Bonner's Hill Road, where she lost him again. She never would have found him if the Bupps hadn't called the state police, she told me.

Buddy's back home again, contentedly munching grain and roaming the barnyard despite the popular notion that once a calf learns to escape the fence, there's no keeping it in. Last I heard, the cute little bull had changed his wild ways and never run away again. Butter wouldn't melt in his mouth.

*To this day, John Holder remembers his runaway
calf. As it turned out, Buddy developed an incorri-
gible disposition and was difficult to manage even
after becoming a steer. "If I hadn't put a ring in his
nose, he'd have killed somebody," John recently told
me. As a result, the Holders sent him to market
nearly a year earlier than they'd planned.*

Rush Hour
June 1990

Pity the poor commuter: rush-hour traffic, diesel
fumes, chugging carburetors, smog, and groaning air con-
ditioners. Every day my husband drives to and from the
city over miles of concrete where heat waves rise even in
winter from the internal combustion engines of countless
commuters traveling from the suburbs to the town.

Not me.

One of the best parts of my day job is the 29-mile drive
to the office and home again. My office building is in rural
Franklin County, Pennsylvania, on a small college campus next to the Michaux State Forest. One night as I
drove from work toward the main road just at dusk, a
great-horned owl glided from the trees to perch on a telephone pole right in front of me. I stopped the car and
stared at the bird for a good two minutes. It was immense,
majestic, with riveting eyes and ear tufts curling from its
head like horns.

"Wouldn't see that in town," I sighed.

While my mate battles the hordes of drivers let out of
their glass edifices by the stroke of five, hell bent to hit
the road before the others, clutching their steering wheels
in death grips, jockeying to avoid the buses and semis,
bopping to the refrains of Motley Crue, I wind my way
over hill and dale with no greater aggravation than slow-

moving farm tractors or flatbeds groaning with apple crates.

Sun at my back, morning and afternoon, I drive to and from the hazy ridges of South Mountain, where the foothills ripple with fruit trees, and here and there a white church steeple reaches into the blue-gray sky.

For the most part, I take the straight-through path from my house: Cranberry Valley Road to Old Carlisle Road, past Center Mills where the mill is long gone but a man is selling log houses in pieces to be reconstructed, across Route 234 through Biglerville and Arendtsville. Then up and down the roller-coaster hills until I get to the great white-frame round barn and several other classic barns, one red, one white, with Victorian gingerbread and cupolas. I like to think that this terrain is like the round barn, with no corners where devils can hide.

Still, a few wild hairs sneak in from time to time, and during the last few years a number of massage parlors have congregated along this woodsy stretch of U.S. Route 30, the Lincoln Highway, where Chief Split Cloud, now gone to the happy hunting ground, built his longhouse years ago. "Live Dancers," one of them advertises with flashing colored lights.

It serves to amuse me till I turn left at Caledonia and into the Michaux Forest. Here the air is always piney-smelling from the towering white pines that overtook the hills after turn-of-the-century charcoal burning had slashed the first growth, denuding the landscape, some say, all the way to Harrisburg.

Some evenings, especially in summer, I take the long, cool route home, up over the Piney Mountain Summit via Route 234, where a sign says the elevation is 1,350 feet, and down into the Narrows. To get there I must go through Buchanan Valley, past the old Jesuit mission where the Catholic church already has a sign out announcing its August picnic. There are other signs: "Brown Eggs for Sale"; "Eternity is Forever, Heaven or Hell"; and "Scenic Valley Tour." It is a beautiful valley, and lots of Dillons have settled here: for a stretch, every other mailbox seems to say "Dillon" till I get to Bill's Place.

Bill's Place is a small white bungalow with window boxes full of geraniums and tiny American flags. Beer and lunch are announced on a Coca-Cola sign, and there is an old Amoco gas pump in the drive and a lit neon Budweiser sign in the window. But I have never seen anyone going in or out.

Then comes Strasbaugh's road stand, where I stop for strawberries and some talk.

"Nice day, isn't it?" observes the elderly gentleman in charge. "S'posed to get pretty nasty tonight....What kinda car's that?"

I get back in the Volkswagen and drop down into the cool, green narrow passage between these ridges of the South Mountain. On my right I hear the rushing Conewago Creek and all along the roadsides the rustling of lush, ferny growth.

It's a long drive, but it sure beats rush-hour traffic.

In 2004, artist Wayne Fettro completed a series of murals on barns and building walls along our stretch of the Lincoln Highway, depicting early motorists on the country's first coast-to-coast highway, constructed in 1913. Part of a state and federal project to promote the Lincoln Highway Heritage Corridor, Fettro's murals appear in Adams, Franklin, Fulton, Bedford, Somerset and Westmoreland counties. Other artists have painted murals in additional Pennsylvania counties and other states that the historic highway traverses.

153

Triplets!
February 1992

February is all but behind us and there are new lambs in the barn. Spring can't be far away.

You'd think we'd be jaded by now. Every year for the past dozen, we've witnessed the birth of sheep and goats in the marginal old structure, its walls and roof patched with tar paper and scavenged signboards, doors hanging slightly askew on bent hinges.

The animals never minded the winter quarters and, in fact, seemed to enjoy their respite from the fields. But this year promised to be dull with just one bred ewe. Like us, our stock is aging, and after two years of drought and an empty corncrib, we had neither the courage nor the sustenance to bring too many babies into the world. So only Spunky, a bottle baby we hand-fed after her own mother rejected her at birth some years back, was allowed to visit the ram.

This year, it was my mate's turn to play midwife. "We've got a lamb!" he announced when he came in from morning chores before leaving for his job in the city.

"You go on ahead," he pushed, knowing that a meeting arranged months before was on my work schedule. He grabbed the bottle of iodine and some soft, clean rags and changed into jeans and an old shirt.

I was gulping a glass of orange juice when he dashed back into the kitchen and yelled, "It's twins—get me some more rags." Although Spunky was, herself, a triplet, she had been giving birth to singles for three or four years, and this never disappointed us because the lambs were always big and healthy and, therefore, survived at a better rate than multiples. Furthermore, she was a good mother and seemed to relish her work.

I got the rags, a threadbare towel and the back of an

old flannel shirt, and had just finished calling my husband's secretary to let her know he'd be late, when he ran in the door once more, proclaiming, "Three! It's triplets—we've got three!"

"What are we going to do?" I lamented. Twins, I was sure she could handle. Triplets were a bit much and under ordinary circumstances meant that one would be a bottle baby.

"I don't know," he said, "but you can't worry about it now. You've got to get to work." Without a backward glance at my barn boots, I climbed in the car and took off, already late for my meeting.

With the farm nearly an hour away, a quick drive home over lunch hour was impossible; my choice of career over my former life weighed heavily on me. After lunch, I called him at his office. "What did we have—boys or girls?" I wanted to know.

"I don't know," he marveled. "Every time I went out, there was another one. I was so excited, I never looked." Everything seemed fine when he left, he said. All three lambs were standing and appeared healthy, though small. He'd cleaned the mother's udder and made sure her milk was down. Still, one of us had always been there to check on the newborns every hour or so. Each little one had, in turn, latched on to one of Spunky's two teats for an initial drink of colostrum, the magical first milk that provides newborns with warmth and energy and doses them with all sorts antibodies, vitamins and protein. A bottle baby was out of the question at this point in our lives, John reasoned, ever the unconvincing pragmatist. He, too, could not afford to miss work but he could end his workday by mid-afternoon. "Spunky's a good mom, and we just have to trust her. Till we get home, they'll all be alive or they won't."

My heart sank. I called up apparitions of limp newborns and reconsidered my decision to put business first. Maybe I should have canceled the meeting and stayed home today, I worried. An old recurring nightmare about a baby I'd failed to properly nourish came to mind. Then the phone rang with a call from a major donor, and I didn't have time to fret till I climbed in the car again after dark. Seldom had the commute seemed so long. When at last my headlights broke around the bend and into the driveway. I reached under the seat for a flashlight and fumbled my way up to the barn to open the top half of the double door into Spunky's stall.

"Where are they?" I panicked, spying at first only the new mother's immense body, cushioned all over with dense cream-colored merino fleece.

There under her belly were six pairs of feet and three shiny-eyed half pints—two black and one white with spotted ears—two girls and a boy, I would later learn. One nursed, its tail wiggling frantically. All were warm and well when I tiptoed in beside them.

"Triplets," I jubilantly announced to the night. "It's almost spring."

Taking a full-time job away from the farm in 1989 proved a wrenching experience for me. With both our sons away at college, I had no practical reason to remain so mightily rooted at home—except during lambing season. New lambs gambol into the dark arms of winter, all baas and curly fleece. They allow themselves to be held and, mistaking you for their mother, will nuzzle the tender spots behind your ears. Lambing is an exercise in optimism not to be missed.

Fifteen Pounds of Blue, Twisted Steel
May 1995

"Fifteen pounds of blue, twisted steel." That's how Mitch's master, Bill Daniels, describes his 9-year-old Jack Russell terrier who is one of three of the breed owned by his family.

When I asked how old he is, my friend Teeta, Bill's wife, looked it up in the family birthday book, where the dogs are listed alongside the children and grandchildren. Mitch's birthday, she told me, is in June. Little did she know when she brought the cute little pup home that day nearly nine years ago that he'd turn into a world-class varmint hunter.

Most people who watch the TV show *Frasier* know the Jack Russell breed in the character of Eddy, Frasier Crane's family pet, but Jack Russells also appear in TV commercials that call for little dogs capable of jumping over a big dog's back or performing other ambitious tricks. Mitch's big sister, Maggie, sits up, dances, and rolls over and plays dead when anyone points a finger at her and says "bang, bang."

While the TV Eddy is a broken coat, or mixed smooth- and rough-coat, Mitch is a smooth-coat Jack Russell, mostly white, with a brown tip on his tail, a brown spot on his back, brown ears, a white blaze on his face, and big brown eyes.

What sets him apart is that when instinct calls, Mitch becomes a 15-pound killing machine. And the object of his attention is usually a woodchuck.

"He's cost us a lot of money," Teeta says. It was most likely a woodchuck that gave Mitch the mysterious liver disease he acquired a year or so ago when he needed a liver biopsy, a trip to a well-known veterinary hospital in Philadelphia, and more than $900 in medical care. His lower lip has been severed by razor-sharp woodchuck teeth more times than the family can count—so many that they've quit taking him in to have it stitched shut.

Mitch's usual tactic is to chase his prey—most often snakes, rats or woodchucks—into holes, under sheds and through tunnels, catch them and shake them silly. Once, he cornered a woodchuck in the drain pipe of the family's pond and refused to come out until it died.

A few months ago, a woodchuck almost cost Mitch his life. He was missing for two whole days—disappeared. Normally, when Mitch takes off, he returns within a day. This time the family thought he'd been stolen until their youngest son, Jon, heard him bark just once. Jon went to the pasture next to the pond to search an area where he knew a community of groundhogs lived in a network of burrows and tunnels. Listening at the holes, he eventually located Mitch by the sound of his breathing. In the midst of the chase, Mitch had apparently got himself to an exit hole, but in trying to dig his way to the woodchuck, he shoved so much dirt under his belly that he got stuck. Try as he may, the dog could move neither backward nor forward.

"All we could see was his nose and ears, and we couldn't even see that at first," says Teeta.

Jon, a spelunker, decided to make use of his training in cave rescues. Grabbing his caver's shovel, a short entrenching tool, he dug a hole three feet straight down, parallel to the exit hole. He put his shirt over the exit hole so the dirt wouldn't fall on the dog. It took a full hour of digging for Jon to get to Mitch. Finally, he reached in and pulled his pet out by his hind feet.

Then, according to Teeta, Mitch jumped up, shook the dust off his short-haired coat, trotted to some adjacent bushes to relieve himself, and headed right back into the woodchuck hole. "I reached down, grabbed him by his tail and took him in the house," Teeta laughs.

When Mitch isn't out hunting woodchucks, he's the constant companion of Teeta's 88-year-old mother, cuddling on her lap in the family's sun room, carefully following her about the house so as not to get underfoot, hanging on her every word."She calls him 'Mitchie,' and she feeds him when we're not looking," my friend tells me. "We built an apartment for her when she came to live with us and made arrangements for all her medical needs, but the best thing we could have done for her was to have Mitch."

Mitch—15 pounds of pure love and blue, twisted steel.

Mitch's reputation lives on, though he and Teeta's mother have both passed away.

Diamond in the Rough
August 2003

"Diamond in the rough," the classified ad read.

I was sure this was another wild goose chase, but he would not be deterred. Now he's the happiest man alive. Never mind that it was not inspected. Never mind that he had to use a screwdriver to start it. Never mind that most men his age have long ago outgrown their fantasies about having their very own little red dump truck.

We'd been down this road before. Back when he first began hankering for a vehicle that would handle more than your average pickup truck, he came upon a bargain; and then a dump truck that didn't exactly meet the criteria for roadworthiness came to live at our house. All I could figure was that he felt sorry for the vehicle and the previous owner knew a sucker when he saw one.

"You did WHAT?" I gasped. "They should have paid someone to haul this thing away!"

The floorboards were so badly rusted that you could

see the road. It coughed and wheezed and smoked and ran—never on the road—only on occasion. The cab had been infested with mice and smelled foul. Adding insult to injury, it came with an equally onerous, unworthy pickup truck of the ilk known hereabouts as a "field truck," the cab of which was supposed to be a replacement for the dump's riddled front end.

It was a disaster from the start, but for the most part he kept it hidden behind one of several barns on our property. Rarely did I have to explain how I continued to be married to a man of such questionable taste.

Certainly, the diamond is an improvement. For the uninformed, let me explain that purchasing a secondhand dump truck is an educational experience. Initially, I simply ignored the return calls from people with large vehicles for sale; however, I soon observed that even the least of these vehicles does not come cheap. Before long, every man who knows him was offering tips on dump trucks for sale at various locations throughout the tri-state area.

"Hi, Bill," I'd say when a like-minded friend called to relay detailed information on a two-ton Chevy with an automatic transmission and an eight-foot bed, accompanied by a phone number with an unrecognizable area code.

For the most part, I was safe. Anything that sounded fairly reliable was well beyond his pocketbook. He'd drive miles to look at these vehicles, come home and stew until people of more legitimate purpose—contractors, small municipalities, professional haulers—bought them.

Exactly what, you might wonder, was his purpose? It's an obvious question to which he'd smile and give variously vague answers. Our insurance agent wryly noted that most people do not buy a dump truck to drive to the grocery store.

"It's just that I've always wanted one," he finally admitted to me. I'd heard this tune before.

With a recent paint job and a better body and engine, this truck was an improvement over the first one. However, it did not bode well when, on the initial drive home, the diamond overheated and had to be pulled off the road more than once.

A natural mechanic, my mate fussed over her, repairing the thermostat and ignition, replacing a light bulb, and having the truck inspected.

Until recently, I'd never thought to ask him why the owner was selling the diamond.

"Oh, that," he smiled. "The guy got a divorce."

The diamond continues to make occasional runs to a farm 10 miles south for horse manure, but she remains rough and needs repairs before, during and after almost every trip.

Chapter 5
Home to Foster Kids, a Country Doctor, and Bangers and Mash

ᏝᏝ

Times are changing. Traffic heading north out of Baltimore and Washington, D.C., is on the increase well past the northern Maryland border and into Gettysburg. Fruit growers hereabouts, squeezed by global competition, are beginning to sell their orchards to outside developers, and houses with paved streets now appear with increasing regularity on acreage that until recently had been cultivated. People are coming here looking for a little piece of land they can call home just as my husband and I once did. I want these new outlanders to hear the voices and touch the fabric of those who came before them and to carry a little of our rock-solid Adams County wisdom into the unknowable future.

Room for One More
October 1981

Pauline Miller never married but she had 27 children. In 1942, Pauline and her brother Bill wrote to county officials asking for two "welfare children" and telling them that the family's 12-room house, which had seen nine Miller children come and go, seemed empty now.

"My youngest brother is in the army and, since he went, my mother, who is 74, is so lonely. We thought children would cheer her up a little. We have plenty to eat and plenty of room," Pauline wrote. Until her death in

1976, Pauline gave love and hope to 27 children who came to her as youngsters and stayed on into adulthood.

"At last they began to feel as if they were home," observed Lois H. Boenau, caseworker supervisor for the Adams County Children and Youth Services. In a recent interview, Boenau said, "It all goes back to her being an accepting, positive person. She didn't make judgments. She recognized children's feelings, and she never criticized their birth families."

When Charles "Butch" Aughinbaugh was three years old, he and his brother went to live with "Aunt Pauline and Uncle Bill," as he calls them. "I lived there 22 years and I'll always consider them my mother and father. They never had as much as other people had, but we kids had an awful lot....No matter what the circumstances, they would never turn anybody away."

In a written report, one caseworker observed that although their surroundings were simple, "These children are taught to accept the things in life which are most meaningful. They are active in the church and observe holidays in the old-fashioned way."

At Christmas and Thanksgiving all the nine original brothers and sisters and their families gathered to feast with the foster children on a meal that Pauline had stayed up till the wee hours of the morning preparing. "She really gave her heart out," Aughinbauch says, all year long and especially on holidays. The two might have as many as eight children in the old house at one time.

Although they were never asked to labor on the farm, each child had his or her chores to do. Some learned how to milk the cow, others fed the chickens. "I had a goat named Elvis," Aughinbaugh remembers.

Like his older foster brothers and sisters, Aughinbaugh decided to quit school when he was old enough. "Aunt Pauline came and talked to me," he says. They

agreed that he would return to high school, and he became the first of her foster children to graduate. "We were
really close. If I had any problems, I always went to
her....Wherever I went, she always went with me." Aunt
Pauline was the proud mother at his graduation and his
wedding. "I'm married now, have two kids, and whatever
I have or hope to be, I owe it to them," the 34-year-old says
of his foster parents.

Pauline continued to open her home to foster children
even after the death of her brother, who had quit his
teaching career to stay home and run the 100-acre farm.
When she died quite suddenly at the age of 69, Aughinbauch and some of the others purchased a plaque to hang
in the old Upper Bermudian Church they knew as youths
on the farm. "In loving memory of Pauline H. Miller and
William R. Miller, who devoted their lives to their foster
children. They loved us," it reads.

More than once an errant parent dropped tearful children on Pauline's doorstep in the middle of the night. Her
youngest brother, Harold "Bud" Miller, and a nephew who
lives nearby tried to talk her out of keeping them, observing that she was getting too old to can, bake and look
after foster children. But the children were what kept her
going.

A popular misconception is that foster parents take in
welfare children for the room and board money the state
allots them. In 1953 that allotment amounted to $1.05 per
day. In 1964 it increased to $1.75 and today is $4.25 plus
clothing allowances for regular care—not much when you
consider the appetites of growing children.

Why did she do it? "For love. I don't know any other
reason," said Lois Boenau. Pauline Miller never graduated from high school, and she never left the family farm,
but she knew the simple truth of love that made life a positive, happy thing for children who had smiled little be-

fore they came to her door. And she gave them hope and faith.

When Butch Aughinbaugh left the farm to start adult life, he left with his own family Bible, given to him by Pauline, who wrote a poem in it he never forgot:

"Faith is more than just a word./It's a feeling deep and true/That with every passing hour/Hope is learned anew./Faith means having courage/To know as days go by/That just as long as Faith lives on/Then Hope can never die."

Pauline Miller's house and outbuildings, still in the Miller family, stand just down the road from our place.

Bessie's Windows
August 1984

Red geraniums always flowered in the green-shaded window of her green-tinged wooden house. Passersby and neighbors along Cranberry Road were fascinated with the place. Overgrown by an ancient boxwood hedge and gnarled cedars, its yellow clapboards and green gingerbread trim had long ago faded to a moss-colored patina that also washed the adjacent outbuildings, a carriage house, gazebo and barn. They seemed to lean on each other, arm-in-arm, resisting the enemy, Time.

It was Bessie Spangler's house; her name was on the mailbox and all the neighbors knew how she had come there as a bride. Her husband long since dead, we used to see her in the summertime trimming the hedge or sitting on the porch. We always intended to stop and see her on our way to somewhere, but there never was time.

In the front room stood a player piano that she played for anyone who happened by—friends, neighbors, even door-to-door salesmen, people say. As a young woman, she had been a piano teacher. "I play by notes," Bessie eventually told me. "I play by hand." A while back, she put all the paper rolls in a box in the attic. They got dusty just sitting around and, besides, "If you want to play the rolls, then you have to pump," she said. The songs were in her head then and still are: "In the Good Old Summer Time," "Let Me Call You Sweetheart," "Good Ol' Time in Georgia."

One snow-frosted Sunday in January, a fire crept up on Bessie and swallowed the middle of her house. The room where her piano stood now has blue sky and clouds for a ceiling. The red geraniums are ash, and the green-shaded window where they bloomed is scorched and boarded. Like the windows, Bessie's mind also is boarded—shut against the accident of time and fate that took her house and her world away.

Born on April 12, 1890, Bessie soon will celebrate her 94th birthday. But this year, for the first time in more than 70 years, she won't celebrate it in her own house. "I had one sister, Zula, but she's passed away this long while, and she had no children either, so I'm all alone," Bessie tells me, recalling how her husband, himself an only child, was not inclined to hear the patter of little feet.

A time machine might just as well have whooshed Bessie into the 21st century. Spare and healthy, her clear eyes sparkle when she remembers heirloom tales of how her aunt put horses in the cellar to hide them from Confederate soldiers. And she tells of how, near the turn of the century, she and her husband, Ervin, came to live with his parents in the house on Cranberry Road. "We added rooms on," she says. Then the shades are drawn and the past becomes the present.

"His people's things are all settin' there the same as when they lived…There's an eight-piece bedroom set there, you know. It's a light oak and has a big band of

167

flowers painted on the headboard. I keep the bed made up for anybody to get right in and sleep," she chatters. Reality, for Bessie, is only what it was. The fire is just a misplaced dream.

Yet even nightmares have their happy endings. Bessie now lives with her two cousins—Gertie, 92, and Maude, 93—along with Gertie's son and his wife in a cozy old house near the county line. For the present, her present remains a dream. But Bessie remembers the songs of yesterday.

"What was that one that Erv hated so?" Maude laughs. "I remember, once he got up and went out when you were playin' it."

"Maybe it was 'Yankee Doodle.' He hated to hear me play that," Bessie chuckles. The three carry on an animated afternoon conversation while many of their younger counterparts listlessly lounge in front of daytime TV.

Reminded that they all predate the radio as well as television, they remember the times they first saw a car. "We pretty near broke our necks lookin'....You could hear it comin' up the hill—it was an old chain drive, and we run up to the window to see it," Maude recollects.

"Now nobody looks for a car. Now there's too many," Bessie observes and turns back to her paper. Every day she reads the newspaper and sometimes the Bible.

Gertie pulls on a sweater and steps outside to the woodpile and mailbox. She returns to throw a few logs in the Ashley stove and divvies up today's copy of *The Gettysburg Times*, a section for each.

"Now they've got motorcycles and everything else," Maude continues over the Living section.

"Yes, and airplanes," Gertie replies.

"I never been up in an airplane. Have you?" Bessie pipes.

"No, I never been up in no airplane," says Gertie. "We

used to have a Model-T Ford."

The talk turns back to horses. Bessie used to keep horses, she says, "but not since my husband's dead. I don't have no horses or buggy."

"It was a two-horse farm. That's what they used to call it," notes Gertie.

"Yeah, that's what we always had—two horses—when my husband farmed it." Bessie smiles. She sees me check my wristwatch.

"I have a watch, too, but I don't wear it for everyday. Then, when I go away, I forget to put it on." Bessie doesn't need a watch. Any time she wants, she can sing the old songs and see red geraniums blooming in the window.

A Cape Cod sits on the spot once occupied by Bessie's house.

Smith Big-a-Roo
June 1986

Outside, black cherries hang on the trees in giant handfuls.

"I-reene...Irene." Inside, eighty-year-old John Marks calls to his wife from the outkitchen where bags of odds and ends hang from a ceiling beam and quart boxes sit in neat stacks on a table. It's wonderfully cool here on this bright June day, and John is resting in a chair after the morning's work. Irene hasn't heard him over the radio playing old standards in the kitchen.

I have come for cherries.

"Irene!"

"Sorry, I didn't hear you." She wipes hands as she leaves simmering pots to open the screen door, smiling. "Dinner's at 11:30, ya know."

It's picking season now, and every day sees six, seven

or more plates set around the table for the big midday meal Irene cooks for her family and the help. Today she's fixed a dish of hamburger, macaroni, potatoes and home-canned tomato juice seasoned with onions. A kettle of water sputters on the stove, waiting for roasting ears she has taken from the freezer. On the crowded kitchen counter sits a glass pitcher full of homemade grape juice.

John was just six years old when his family moved to this 105-acre farm in the foothills of the South Mountain. It was 1912 then. In 1933, he married Irene and brought her home.

Through the window at her kitchen sink, Irene still looks out on one of the grandfather fruit trees on the farm. Smith Big-a-Roo, it is called, named for the mammoth sweet black cherries—each one nearly as big as a half-dollar—it faithfully produces. Its trunk is as wide as an elephant, and the shiny gray bark of its fat branches is cracked and gnarled like the skin of an old pachyderm's legs. One of the limbs has broken under the weight of this year's crop.

We walk outside for my cherries, which their 13-year-old grandson, Andy, and his friend are sorting. "They're not as good this year as some," observes Irene, pitching a less than perfect specimen while I wonder how much better cherries can possibly be.

Jane Marks has just chugged up the steep driveway with a pickup truck full of strawberries—the last of the season. "A lot of people say they despise pickin' strawberries," she tells me, "but I like it." Jane is married to Clair Marks, youngest of John and Irene's three children. She opens the pickup cap, releasing a rush of strawberry air from a bed of red fruit, still warm from the fields, and we all agree that there is nothing on earth to equal the smell.

In his early 40s, Clair works a regular job, afternoon shift, as a computer operator. He, Jane and their children,

Andy and Janice, live nearby. Their summer days are spent here on the farm with his parents.

On the heels of strawberries and cherries will come plums, pears, peaches, green beans, apples and potatoes. Most of these Clair markets to local stores, peddling a few to neighbors. When the cherry picking is done, the other fruit crops will require thinning and spraying. Work continues until hunting season starts in November and resumes with tree pruning in mid-winter.

Ten-year-old Janice looks at me. "How'd you like a tour of the farm?"

How could I resist.

"I can show you the carving tree," she pipes.

"The what?"

"The carving tree—over in the woods."

I agree, and after dinner Janice and her mother give me the tour. We check out a nest of fuzzy baby sparrows in John's ("pap's") tool shed. Along the way, Andy and his friend find a milk snake. We peruse the cherry orchard with its grand variety: black cherries, hanging like grapes in bunches or clustered against the limbs as if they are swarms of bees; sour, pie cherries decorating the green trees like Christmas balls; meaty white cherries for canning; and big white cherries with a rosy cheek, purely for fresh eating. Janice, a born tree climber, plucks prime specimens of each for me to taste and taste and taste.

We walk into a tall woods full of old white pines, ferns and 100-foot tulip poplars until we come to the carving tree. There on the iron bark of an ancient beech are the initials. "R.H.M., 1929"; "C.B.M, 1940"; "C.M., 1963"; "C.E.M." loves J.A.M." in a heart; "J.I.M." and "A.R.M." "There's mine and Andy's," says Janice. It's a tour of four generations—the real fruit of John Marks's trees.

171

John and Irene Marks have long since passed away, and the Marks home place was sold a number of years ago. The new owner keeps chickens and sells fresh eggs.

Bangers and Mash
May 1988

"Hi, Peg. How are you?"

"I've got some green bacon today, dear," Peg Knisely says in her British brogue to a familiar customer. "How's everybody?"

They discuss family as another paper of bacon is weighed out. Green bacon, Peg tells me later, is loin bacon that's been cured then smoked just a little. Like Peg, it's English and not green at all, but rosy and delightfully different. Lester makes it and other specialty items that are sold with Peg's famous pâtés, meat salads, Scotch eggs and steak and kidney pies every Friday and Saturday at the West Shore Farmers Market in Camp Hill.

Peg and Lester Knisely are an unlikely Adams County couple. She grew up in London. "My grandmother cooked for Sir Winston [Churchill]," she says. Her father sold meats and poultry to lords and ladies, including the Countess Tolstoy and her husband, Lord Weirdale, a member of Parliament in the House of Lords. Lester was born here, of Pennsylvania Dutch stock, went to New Jersey as a waterworks engineer and returned some years later to open a meat business with his brother. Peg left a career as a schooled cook in a real-life *Upstairs, Downstairs* mansion to seek her fortune in America, where a friend introduced her to the blue-eyed man she would marry. They have a grown son and grandchildren now, and hundreds of friends who are their customers.

"Lester, dear, can we have some chops please," calls

Joan, their helper, and Lester cuts six beautiful chops from a pork tenderloin with a skinny knife. The day before, I watched him make the sausage they sell as English "bangers," pork and veal sausages in natural sheep casings—fresh pink meat finely ground ("I grind it five times," Lester said.) and mixed with coriander, mace, ginger, a dash of cayenne and white pepper. They're called bangers, Peg explained, "Because they go 'bang' when you cook 'em if you don't prick 'em with a fork." They're served with mashed potatoes—"bangers and mash"—and are common fare in English pubs.

The recipe came from Leslie Chartres, author of *The Saints*, who so missed English sausage when he moved here that he asked *Gourmet* magazine to publish it in hopes someone in the States would take it up. When *Gourmet* learned the Kniselys were making bangers, orders began arriving from New York, California, Texas and Hawaii. In addition, the Knisleys make fennel, sage and plain sausage.

Back of their Adams County shop is Lester's smoke house, a small block structure he built himself. For smoking, he uses only fruitwoods along with hickory and sassafras, and a natural cure of maple syrup, salt, pepper and spices, with no preservatives. Lester doesn't believe in preservatives. Fresh food is living food, he believes: "You can't package something and put it on the shelf for an indefinite time...then it is dead."

But modern lifestyles and the fast food industry have taken a bite out of Lester's business. Much of what he sells is meant to be prepared the old-fashioned way, not microwaved in a plastic bag. Last year, market traffic was slow during the summer months. "Like preparing for a banquet and nobody showed up," he sighs. Still, he offers one-of-a-kind specialties such as English rasher, a wide, lean, utterly delicious bacon made from the whole pork loin.

When Lester trims meats, little fat remains. His sausage is leaner than steak I have cooked and of a different world than the stuff in supermarkets. His beef has real flavor.

"Any trifle today?" asks a customer to whom Peg explains that she's been under the weather for a few weeks. At Christmas market there is always trifle, a classic English dessert that Peg makes from sponge cake, sweet sherry, strawberries, a fresh strawberry gelatin, and a custard of eggs and cream. Topped with whipped cream and almonds, it is a majestic treat.

However, Peg's masterpiece is her pheasant pâté. Served at the Governor's Mansion during the Thornburgh administration, it is fit for a king. In it is "the whole bird, of course [a whole organically grown pheasant], a lot of eggs, imported brandy and Madeira, and all kinds of spices," she beams. Everything is fresh, like the exchange that passes over the counter here every weekend. The whole operation is unique, or as Lester puts it, "kind of an individual thing."

If Lester and Peg Knisely were alive now, they would be chagrined to hear about the current practice of irradiating meat to kill bacteria and extend shelf life.

Doc Flickinger
October 1988

No sign reading "Payment Expected When Services Rendered" ever appeared in Doc Flickinger's office. The average price for an office visit was $8.00—it had been $7.00 until he'd asked for a $1.00 increase a year or so ago—and the charge covered extras such as cold pills, blood pressure medicine, and injections when needed.

William Flickinger came to the country town of York Springs as a general practitioner, a handsome young man fresh from medical school, and he stayed for nearly 50 years. On the first floor of the big white house on Main Street were two examining rooms and a waiting room. He took over the practice of his brother-in-law in 1939, and in 1940 he brought his bride, Josephine, to the quarters upstairs where they would raise their children.

Until a few weeks ago, the light on the Flickingers' front porch had been lit nearly every night for all those years.

"It's like losing a member of your own family," said one of his patients, Jim Decker, when the doctor died. "Doc brought both me and my wife into the world. He was a real country doctor." In fact, the doctor brought several thousand babies into the world, and during busy times had as many as 25 deliveries within the same month until he stopped doing obstetrics later in his practice. In the early days he charged $15 and $20 for home deliveries, says his nurse of 40 years, Cathryn Miller. It cost $100 to have a baby in the hospital then, but if no complications were expected, Doc gave his patients the option of having their children at home.

Neva Williams was one of them. On March 4, 1947, she had a snow baby. It was 3 a.m. when Neva's husband, Roy, had to awaken a neighbor to get the doctor by phone. "We didn't have a phone then," she explains. They lived on a dirt road that blowing snow had drifted shut. "Roy met him and brought him in, four miles, on a tractor. Thank the Lord, the baby arrived safe and sound, and Dr. Flickinger spent the rest of the night on our couch." He delivered all six of the Williamses' children.

One woman's newborn came so fast, Doc ushered it in on her kitchen table, Mrs. Flickinger remembers. Impressed by this speedy delivery, the woman's husband asked, "Is that all there is?" Another home birth was for Jeanne and Wendell Lehman. It was a rainy Saturday when Jeanne called the doctor. He joked, "Let's hurry and have this baby, I want to get home and watch *Gunsmoke*," she says. But he never hurried anyone, especially new babies.

Three of his deliveries occurred in the farmhouse where I now live. Romaine Miller, who had 16 children in her time, lived here for 30 years. In the wooden steps to our second story are hollows worn by her family's feet. Her husband, Alton, was a steelworker.

"Dad worked away, and when Mom would call the doctor—she'd send us next door to use Grover Smith's crank phone—he'd always come out," says her son Richard. "When we moved to the farm, things weren't always easy. Once we were quarantined: there was three of us down with scarlet fever....Doc would say, 'I'm not worried. Just pay me when you can.'"

He never went to church much, but reserved Sunday mornings for house calls and often took his dog along in the car. My neighbor Nellie Riley doctored with him for 49 years. "I never called that he didn't come," she says. "He stayed with my mother one night till two o'clock in the morning." The charge for a house call was $10. "We didn't just lose a doctor," observes Nellie, "we lost a good friend."

In 1950, Doc Flickinger made the newspaper when he installed a short-wave radio, a Radiophone, in his car to help him get to patients faster. However, as the years passed, his office saw little change. "He never forgave me for painting this wood," said Mrs. Flickinger when I visited the office recently. In one examining room, she'd had the woodwork painted ivory. In the other, the trim remains the original dark oak, with an oak-mantled fireplace on the outside wall. On his desk sits an old mercury blood pressure cuff in a walnut box. A vision chart hangs on one wall; adjacent to it is an ancient scale and a worn leather-padded examining table. It was nothing, she recalled, for their dog to come bounding in to greet a patient.

"I didn't mind," his wife smiled, when I asked about all the years she'd been there, too, answering his phone, sitting up nights. "Family doctors are pretty important.... Now I have to find one, too."

Michael Daniels, who eventually became my family doctor, took over much of Doc Flickinger's practice after his passing. Cathryn Miller, Doc's nurse, came with the practice and worked in Daniels's Mount Holly Springs office until just before her death in 2008.

Maybelle's Place
February 1989

It is 7:30 on a Monday morning and talk over the green Formica counter at Maybelle's concerns hunting camps, the weather, apples, and a murder. If they don't know about it down at Maybelle's, it hasn't happened yet, say the locals.

Maybelle—the accent is on the second syllable—is the proprietor of Bucher's Restaurant on the square in Bendersville, a town with a bank, a grocery store, a cider mill, an undertaker and no stoplights, where less than 540 people are engaged primarily in fruit growing or related agricultural industries. Back in 1813 Maybelle's was called the Elk Horn Hotel; the stone—walled building is on the site of the original log tavern. In 1952, Maybelle Bucher Davis and her husband bought the restaurant from her mother, Mrs. Annie Bucher. Less than 10 years later, Maybelle was widowed; she's been tending customers on her own ever since.

"Told ya we weren't even gonna get a broom snow," says one of the patrons to nobody in particular. "We don't get no big snows like we used to," he offers, alluding to old rumors that someone—big fruit growers, the federal government or Communists, depending on the nature of your suspicions—is seeding the clouds or otherwise trying to manipulate the weather.

"What happened at that fire down there?" he asks a fellow seated on one of the counter stools sipping coffee, a snuff can bulging from his back pocket. At various points in the morning, conversation has also included the proper temperature for keeping apples in controlled atmosphere storage (34 degrees for MacIntosh, 30-31 degrees for other varieties), the decay of New York City (everybody watched *60 Minutes* on TV last night), and a recent killing in which a young woman allegedly stabbed her boyfriend (he wasn't from around here).

Maybelle's place and Bendersville sit at the eastern base of South Mountain, the beginning of the southern division of the Appalachians. Apple orchards lace the foothills and creep up the mountainsides as each year more and more acres are cleared for cultivation. Yet there's something of the ridge runner in most folks here, and the mountain's hollows offer hiding places to both men and beasts.

"There's still a big buck down there in the valley where ya can't get to," observes a customer as the talk turns to hunting. "Got these new shoes at Sears. Got 'em for half price...I can even hunt in 'em," he beams.

Mary Taughinbaugh, a sprightly 76-year-old who's been at Bucher's Restaurant since 1944, waits on customers. Another Maybelle, Maybelle Finfrock, is the cook.

Maybelle, herself, sits like a queen in the last booth next to the counter and holds court, passing the time of day with friends who drop in for breakfast. "You need your friends," she says, her face to the door so she sees every-one who comes and goes. She was one of 10 children—eight boys and two girls—who grew up on a small farm near here. "We're all born in the same house, the same bed, the same room and the same daddy," she likes to tell folks. "Not many people can say that."

I ask about the old photograph of a hunting party on the wall, where a whole family is pictured next to six fat deer hanging on a sturdy cross pole. She tells me how her daddy liked his hunting camp and points out her brother. She raised two daughters here, Maybelle proudly exclaims. Like her mother, she taught her children the value of hon-esty and hard work. They helped in the restaurant even after they went to college, she says; photos of them sit on the television set in the back corner of the dining room.

Memorabilia decorate the restaurant: behind the counter hangs a pair of straw knives used to cut straw and hay from compacted layers in the haymow, crockware and decanters line shelves along the walls, in the back is an old National cash register and a crank phone.

Lunch today—the restaurant is closed evenings—is going to be hog maw, she tells me. Tomorrow it'll be home-made beef pot pie. Also on the menu are chicken `a la king, vegetable soup, and chili. Wednesday, the special is chicken; Thursday, sauerkraut and pork; and Friday, fish or meatloaf platters are $3.00.

"And the mashed potatoes—are they the real thing?" I ask.

"Yessir! We don't have the other kind," she answers. Everything at Maybelle's is real.

After Maybelle's death and several changes in own-ership, one of which resulted in a short-lived at-tempt at an upscale cafe with matching prices, the restaurant again became known as the Elk Horn.

Jacoby's Chair Factory
October 1989

Wood chips pile up in drifts inside Jacoby's Chair Factory. They cushion the feet, hush the noise and fill the place with a bouquet of cherry, poplar, birch and pine.

A half century or more ago, in and around the crossroads village of Heidlersburg, Pennsylvania, chairmaking was a booming business, a cottage industry that kept many families going during the Great Depression. The area was famous then for producing woven-seated porch rockers, outdoor furniture of the time before aluminum folding chairs. Now Jacoby's Chair Factory is all that's left to remind locals of those days gone by.

Orville Jacoby's father, Orville Sr., started the business then, selling porch rockers for seventy-five cents each to various wholesalers.

"Truckloads of 'em went out of here when I was a kid. That's all I saw was chairs," observed Hazel Jacoby, who works in the chair factory with Orville and another of her brothers, Glenn. "There were 12 of us, six boys and six girls." Still another brother has his own chair business in nearby Biglerville, away from the home place.

Today the Jacobys make a lot more than chairs: tables, dressers, beds and cabinets, among other things. "Most of our work is cabinets," observed Orville when I asked him about their sign in which an illustration of an old ladder-back serves for the *h* in the word *chair*. "But I'll never change the name." Orville moved back home and took over the business more than 20 years ago, after his father died. Later, he and Glenn formed a partnership.

All around the shop hang wooden patterns for chair backs, seats, arms and rockers. Sawdust festoons everything. "Wait a minute," pushed Orville, blasting with an air gun the plank-bottom chair I wanted to try.

"Sits nice."

"That's an arrow-back," he smiled. "Trouble is, you get 'em to sit too comfortable, then you eat too much."

Today they make eight different kinds of chairs—traditional ladder-backs, short ladder-backs, fiddle-backs, harp-backs, bootjack-backs and others—all with plank-bottom seats. Orville laughed when he told me about the couple who couldn't agree on which kind to get for their table and went home with eight different chairs.

Glenn's son David now has a shop of his own just down the road and weaves the old split wood seats and backs just as his grandfather did. Sometimes one of her father's chairs comes back for repair of the seat or a rung, Hazel said. Often, it belongs to someone who has acquired it at a sale and is surprised to learn it was made here.

On a shelf in the back of the shop are oak and cherry pedestals that David has turned from octagons made with eight pieces of wood, splined and glued together. Orville's son Donald, who has a job with Westinghouse, also works in the shop along with his teenage son Jesse in his free time. Jesse is the fifth generation woodworker in the family, Hazel observed.

Along with plank-bottom chairs, one of their most popular items is still the deacon's bench, which Orville Sr. began making after a time. The top of one hangs porch-swing style from the ceiling. Like most of their chairs it is made from poplar, a favorite wood of the Jacobys' due to its strength and ability to take a stain. Finished, the deacon's benches sell for from $160 for a three-foot bench to $495 for the 10-foot model, with an extra charge for hardwoods.

Many of their customers want pieces that appear old, Orville said, recalling one kitchen cabinet. "The lady said she wanted it to look 130 years old," he said, so his son set about distressing the piece. "He worked at it with a chain and carved into it with a pocket knife. He even used bent nails in it. 'You'd better hold off on that,' I told him. The woman called up and said that was exactly what she wanted."

In the last 20-some years, only three of the Jacobys' chairs have come back for seat repair, Orville offered. "We don't advertise much," Hazel said. "If you treat people fair and give 'em good quality, they talk *for* you."

Following the death of his brother, Orville Jacoby passed away in 2007 and the chair factory closed. Hazel turned 80 in 2009 and is retired. Glenn's son David still builds furniture in a shop next door to the original chair factory.

Shearing
June 1991

We wouldn't think of having anyone but Mark Gutshall shear our sheep and, even if we tried, we probably couldn't get another shearer to come out for our small flock. It hardly pays him to make the trip to our place from his, the next county over, but he's been shearing our animals and those of a friend a few miles down the road for 12 years now—he goes to her place first and ours last—and the annual event has become a tradition for all of us.

It was late in the season when Mark got to our place this year but, with summer having arrived early, he'd had his hands full making hay and planting grain crops in addition to milking a herd of dairy cows, morning and night.

From inside the barn arose a great yammering and clambering. Wool dampened from stray thundershowers doesn't shear well, so we'd had our animals penned for most of the week and they thought this unexpected bit of hubbub meant an extra dip from the grain barrel for them. Instead, we yanked them from the stalls one at a time, pushing, pulling each obstinate bulk toward the barnyard where Mark had laid his oily tarp on the dry ground and waited with his large pair of electric shears, hoof snips, a squirt bottle full of oil, and antiseptic gel.

Having sent many a reluctant farm animal off to market, I have always believed that they sense real danger from the scents pervading the occasion and are as capable as we of communicating their feelings to one another. By now they know they have nothing to fear from Mark except an occasional nick from his shears in the corpulent folds of their bellies.

Blackie, a small black ram turned brown from the sun was first. "C'mon fella," Mark coaxed, and within seconds the sheep was resting on his hind end, eyes bulging, feet and belly in the air. We laughed, remembering how I fretted the first time I'd seen Mark roll a sheep, fearing that it would die if it lay on its back for even a fraction of a second. In no time at all, the brown fleece was removed and hastily bundled away. (You have to blanket black sheep for a desirable quality of wool.) Blackie's hooves were trimmed and the next customer, a husky old Merino we called Rasputin, was tugged to the tarp for his summer suit.

Mark is at least six feet tall and wiry. This year he had strapped on a pair of leather leggings that made his long, thin legs look like poles and, as he manipulated the immense beast, it occurred to me that, soaking wet with sweat as he was tonight, he was about half the weight of this fat ram. He was just a high school kid when he started shearing our sons' 4-H show lambs; now he farms more than 100 acres and has a family of his own.

In a twinkling, Rasputin was done—Mark having started with a long stroke up the belly "like a zipper" and buzzed away with long deft strokes toward the neck, shoulders, hind quarters and across the back—and the thick yellow fleece lay on the ground, tucked into a fat bundle tied with paper twine.

The fleeces of Rasputin and his offspring provide the best wool in our small flock. Yellow and heavy with lanolin, it felt damp this evening, but Mark said the lanolin made it easy to shear.

"Nothin' like an old Suffolk *yo* (country for *ewe*) in a woven wire fence." He laughed as we pushed Daisy, her ragtag wool rubbed bare in uneven patches, onto the tarp. "She's got half my work done till I get here."

Cleo, the goose, her wings stretched protectively over a nest full of lifeless eggs nearby, pecked at the straw beneath her and stretched her long neck in a menacing motion toward the intrusive activity in her barnyard. "Whatcha need is a gander," Mark advised, tongue in cheek, though we think better of being chased about by an even more ferocious winged beast.

Two more ewes, and we were finished. And we turned the flock, delightedly lighter, out to pasture again. We passed the time of day with a conversation about Mark's new John Deere hat and he unstrapped the leggings and loaded his tools into the battered bed of his pickup.

At $3 a head and $5 for the trip, our shearer had little to show for his journey across the county line this evening. We thanked him profusely, hoping that he would come again next year. Without him we could not continue our backyard operation.

Mark Gutshall made his trek over the county line every spring until our aged animals were mostly buried out in the back pasture and only one old ewe remained.

Hickory Point School Reunion
August 1991

They had a bond, a camaraderie that few youngsters know today. They didn't have to ask, "Who am I?" or "Where do I belong?" They knew.

Every year for the last five, the alumni of Hickory Point have gathered for a reunion at my neighbor Kenneth Bupp's farm. They eat good food from a smorgasbord of covered dishes, show old photographs and remember how it used to be in the one-room school they attended from first through eighth grade. Some are in their eighties now, some in their seventies and sixties, and some little more than fifty. Many never went on to the high school in town, for these were the days before school buses when most families owned only one horse, much less two cars. Some graduated from high school. A few graduated from college.

One went to normal school and came back to teach for eight years at the same one-room school she had attended for eight years; eventually, she earned a master's degree. Grace Garretson laughed, recalling her eight years as a teacher at Hickory Point. "I made a lot of fire and swept floors a lot." She played with the children a lot, too: games such as Tickly High Over, which involved throwing a sponge ball over the school house roof; and Clap In and Clap Out, played indoors on rainy days; or Fox and Geese. In winter the yard behind the school froze over like a pond and the teacher and students skated on it in their shoes. Grace said that it snowed so hard in 1936 that for six weeks she went to school on a bobsled.

"Best teacher I ever had," cried one woman, hugging her.

Hickory Point School was planned at a meeting in Bowers' Tavern in 1838 but not built until 1866, first, because of local opposition to compulsory education and, later, because of the Civil War. Eventually, dozens of one-room school houses dotted the landscape of Adams County. Most had ceased operation by the 1950s, but many of them still stand, as does Hickory Point, closed in 1947 but now a quaintly remodeled home which, word has it, recently sold for "80-couple thousand dollars."

Land for the Hickory Point School was bought from George Group and his wife, Amanda, for $10 per half acre, according to Harold "Bud" Miller, who grew up in a farmhouse just down the road from the one where I now live. Bud started school at Hickory Point with four other children but was the only one in his class by the time he got to sixth grade. When he graduated and passed the high school entrance exam in 1926, he could have quit, according to the law, but he walked the three miles to York Springs High School, along with other children in the neighborhood.

"For four years I walked in there, and in four years I missed two days," Bud declared, hastening to add that there were no snow days for blizzards. "When it snowed hard, we'd line up—do like the wild geese—and the first one would break the snow. Then we'd trade off. The roads would be shut and we'd walk through the fields. And we'd get there."

The school rules were listed on the backs of the report cards when Kenneth Bupp went to eighth grade during the school year of 1941-42. By that time the most important rule seemed to be that regarding compulsory school attendance from ages eight to 18. Parents who didn't comply, the rules admonished, were guilty of a misdemeanor.

But this rule apparently was only loosely enforced. The "big boys"—who never came to school in the fall until after the corn was harvested, took a week off to hunt rabbits and often attended school until they were 18—offered one-room school teachers one of their two biggest challenges. The other was the county superintendent, who gave the exam teachers needed to pass as part of their certification and visited the schools from time to time to check on his charges.

Indoor plumbing was nonexistent hereabouts in those days, and the students pumped drinking water at a nearby farm and carried it back to the school in a stone jug. Mabel Zepp Cashman went to Hickory Point for three years and fondly recalls that stone jug and the school bell her teacher rang. "We had to work together. When it got cold we stood around the stove. The kids today don't have anything like that to remember."

Come summer, signs go up in my neighborhood announcing the Hickory Point reunion at the Bupp farm.

Something About a Porch
July 1993

There's something about a porch. Exposed yet protected, you can sit on your porch on a summer's evening and listen to the katydids, or huddle on it during an afternoon thunderstorm to watch the downpour. When people haul out their gliders and invite their neighbors over for pinochle and iced tea, you surmise a certain mindset—an abandonment of the cares of winter, a celebration of summer.

Traditional old porches are hard to beat, topped by planked ceilings that often are painted sky blue and underpinned by damp crawl spaces fronted by whitewashed wooden lattice that provides the perfect hiding space for any child unafraid of daddy longlegs in the dark. But old-fashioned porches have gone the way of the windmill and the outhouse, replaced by weatherproof Florida rooms and the more convenient patio or the ubiquitous deck. Sad to say, modern life is lived with too few blue-sky porch ceilings and cave-like crawl spaces. And the child who doesn't remember swinging in a hammock under rafters dotted by wrens' nests or crouching in an earthen underbelly during a game of cops and robbers is the poorer for not having had a porch.

This summer we are rebuilding our front porch. After much discussion on a possible relocation of the steps, we decided to restore the old porch to its original appearance in the days when a schoolteacher named John Guise built the house before the end of the last century.

Four porches, counting the balcony, graced the house then. With two of the porches already lost to an enclosing trend that swept this locale in the 1950s, we chose to tear away the cement pad and cement-block steps that had long since replaced the wooden ones and reinstate our traditional front porch. It wasn't as easy as it sounds.

First, my mate rented a jackhammer to break up the cement and mortar. Then we hauled the heavy gray stuff away in wheelbarrows. Buried in it for reinforcement we found old steel cans, cultivator blades, and an ornate steel bedstead. In the meanwhile, we jacked up the front pillars we'd already replaced a few years back.

Finding tongue-and-groove floorboards at a good price proved a challenge, but the greater test was working together again on another home improvement project. "Hold that board a half inch down from the post," he instructed.

"But the board on the other side is three-and-a-half inches from the post," I said.

"Whaddya mean? I told you to make *it* a half-inch."

"No you didn't. I never heard you say that!"

When he was ready to screw in the joists, he discovered that the building supply clerk had sold him nails instead of screws. When it was time to lay the floor, the temperature soared to 100 degrees. "Lotta work for something that's never going to be used," he complained after a full day of perspiration-soaked labor.

Now it is July and, with the renovations halfway finished, I am getting ready to paint. I have plans for the porch, I tell him. I can see Paul's scarlet roses climbing the lattice toward the roof and a pair of Shaker rocking chairs perched at either side of the steps. Of course, there's a pot of geraniums in the middle. I can see us sitting in the chairs, sipping iced tea, listening to the katydids and watching for falling stars on a summer's night.

There's just something about a porch.

Paul's scarlet climbers did bloom nicely against our latticework, but the porch never got enough sun for geraniums. Every Christmas John hangs a lighted Moravian star from the porch roof for me.

The Arendtsville Garage
February 1995

"You can tell this place runs on computers," the man said, tongue in cheek. It was a compliment to the father-and-son team that owns and operates the Arendtsville Garage.

The man, a teacher who lives just across the street, wanted to know what he owed for a gallon of windshield-washer fluid. Neither Glenn nor Loy Hoke could remember the price just off the top of their heads, but ask them about an orchard sprayer they sold in 1974 or any other given year and they could cite minute details about its parts and longevity. The closest thing to a computer in the garage is the electric adding machine on the corner of the counter, just left of the old black telephone and a vintage cash machine.

"One-fifty," Loy said eventually, and the man paid 83-

year-old Glenn, joking about owing him $150 for the gallon jug of blue liquid.

No, the Arendtsville Garage doesn't run on computers.

"I have nothing against computers," drawled Loy, a diminutive man with graying hair, blue eyes, and a trim mustache. "But for us it would mean a lot of big bucks," he said, motioning to the numbered parts bins along the walls of the garage—orchard-sprayer parts on this side, car and truck parts on the other. "Somebody has to pay for that....You'd have to pass it along to the customer.

"We try to treat the customer right—sell them what they should have, not what we've got to sell....The best deal for the best service. A lot of it is, you've got to give good service.

"That's what sold this sprayer here." Loy nodded toward a brand new, stainless steel-tanked Durand-Wayland sprayer that's going to a man in Martinsburg, Virginia. Oddly enough, the sprayer is computerized, he offered, explaining that its mechanism senses the difference between trees and open ground and sprays the exact height and width of the tree.

At a recent horticultural society meeting in Hershey, Loy met a man who remembered buying a sprayer from him years ago. The man now owns a farm in the Hudson River Valley outside New York City, and the sprayer is still running.

The garage is a hangout for locals. On a snowy day, Loy laughed, it's "kind of like a social club." He has just finished talking to an Amish man who has dropped in to consult him—free of charge, of course—about a sprayer the man is considering buying from a fellow named Petey outside Bendersville.

The sprayer business is better than the auto repair business of late. The days of the independent neighborhood garage are numbered, Loy said, lamenting that "Automobiles today are getting so high-tech, you have to go to the dealer for repairs. You can't take a Ford to a GM dealer or a Chrysler to a Buick dealer.

"We build some of our own spray booms and up to 500-gallon sprayers. We build them in our shop." In addition to the Loys, the garage has two mechanics. "We work on tractors and trucks; anything we can get through the door," Loy offered, gesturing toward the old wooden tri-fold garage door. "And if we can't get it through the door, we work on it in the alley."

In 1945, his father bought the garage, an old-fashioned stone-faced block building that had opened in 1922 as a new car showroom where Ford, Chevy, Buick, Oldsmobile and Star automobiles were sold. Designed by farmers, it was "the biggest building that didn't have posts—the first completely trussed building in the area," Loy declared, pointing out the huge beams from which motors were hoisted in the old days and the two-feet-wide boards that sheath the roof. Tool chests line the walls, along with drill presses, a welder and machines used to bore engines.

"May I have one of these?" I asked on my way out, picking up my very own Arendtsville Garage calendar, complete with the Hokes' very own version of technology—a cardboard gas mileage computer that clips to your sun visor.

Though Rudisill's Auto Repair and Towing occupies the old building, Loy Hoke does new sprayer sales and sprayer repairs and service nearby at 135-A Main Street, still known as the Arendtsville Garage.

Chapter 6
Loss, Love and Reconciliation in the Garden of Eden

❦

Prior to the Civil War, the Underground Railway, which carried runaway slaves to freedom, was quite active in Adams County, largely due to its abolitionist Quaker residents. On what was then Quaker land at a place called Yellow Hill not far from Biglerville, former slaves (light-skinned, or "high yellow," it is presumed, giving the place its name) settled and eventually built a church with a hitching rail, a picket fence and a cemetery. It is said that sometime in the 1890s the church was burned down by three white men. Though its tombstones had been removed, you could still see evidence of them in the 1980s, when I was writing for *The Gettysburg Times*.

With Gettysburg as its hub, Adams County has seen its share of good and bad deeds. After all, the bloodiest battle of the Civil War raged here on this beautiful landscape with its orchards and wheat fields and rocks so hard that, according to my geologist friend, Helen Delano, soldiers could not dig trenches at the infamous Devil's Den and other battle sites.

So much in this life is a matter of perspective: contentment or misery; beauty or homeliness; wisdom or ignorance. My coming of middle age has shown me the best and the worst in this exceptional place and its people. There have been calamities, the worst being the burning of an effigy in the wee hours of a September morning in my front yard.

193

Coming full circle—reconciling my life in the fruit belt with its origins in the rust belt—I honestly think that, while prejudice and hate die hard in this world, kindness and love are found in the most unexpected places. I grudgingly accept that change postpones its schedule for no one. One season follows another, children grow up and, if we're lucky, we grow old. I know that loss, even tragic loss, is a natural part of life and appreciate my good fortune in being alive.

9990 Buchenwald
September 1981

I went there for what I expected would be a humorous story about a 21-year-old duck. The aged Katrina had lived for years in the yard of Bruno and Elvira Wolff's unassuming white house south of York Springs. She was their pet, along with four cats and two dogs. Elvira explained to me how she hadn't had the heart to kill Katrina years ago when the duck should have become Thanksgiving dinner, and Bruno told me tales of stray dogs they had adopted. I learned that Mao Tse Tung, an immense cat that understands three languages, presides over the house like a Chinese warlord, and my curiosity was aroused by the couple's love for animals.

As the answers to my questions came, my curiosity grew. "When you pass through the hard life, you learn to love anybody and everything," Elvira said. She had come to this country from Italy in 1950; Bruno came in 1947.

How did they meet?

"During the war. She was working in the underground, and I was hiding," Bruno explained as he recalled his trip to Italy in 1939 after he escaped Buchenwald, a Nazi prison camp.

"Bad times," Elvira shook her head. Along with hundreds of other Jews, Bruno was arrested on *Kristal Nacht*, Crystal Night or the night of broken glass, November 9-10, 1938, when Nazis smashed windows of Jewish-owned buildings and burned the synagogues in Germany.

"My mother called me at the factory," he said, explaining that he had been a shoemaker in the town of Frankfort-Main. "She said, 'There is some trouble in town.' But before I could get home, they had me."

Only men were arrested at that time. Bruno was sent to Buchenwald and his brother to Auschwitz. The economy was bad in Germany, Bruno told me. Years of inflation and unemployment were Hitler's allies in his overthrow of the Weimar Republic. He had to get rid of unemployment, so he started by getting rid of the Jews.

Hadn't they seen it coming, felt the danger? I probed.

"This was the Germany of Einstein, Goethe, Brahms, Schiller, Nietzsche and Freud. Nobody was thinking in the high culture that had been Germany's that this was going to happen. Nobody!" he answered.

What followed seems like a nightmare in which the dreamer searches for a doorway out of the dark. According to Bruno, the Jews taken in that first rush were permitted to leave the concentration camps if they had a ticket of some kind out of Germany and would promise never to return to the country. His mother had secured an affidavit from a Jewish college in Chicago vouching for her sons and had managed to get boat tickets out of the country for the three of them, so he and his brother were permitted to leave the camps after four months. "If you had proof that you could leave—any kind of ticket—you could get out. My ticket was for Shanghai." But after World War II started, time had run out for the Jews, he said. "Who could, went. Who couldn't, it was another story."

Bruno's grandmother died in Theresienstadt, his aunt

in Auschwitz. Aunts, uncles, cousins from Germany and Holland disappeared. A few governments were willing to let Jews enter, but others, like the United States, were very particular and required the refugees to be in top health. Bruno shrugged: "They were looking for people for Australia, but they would only take fair people with blonde hair and blue eyes....If you're looking for an excuse, you're looking for any excuse."

Contrary to popular belief, the Catholic Church did a great deal to aid the Jews, he told me. "If we were saved, we have to thank the Catholic Church for this. The pope officially could do nothing, but many Jews were hidden in the Vatican." En route to Shanghai their boat stopped in Italy. "We were stuck there because the war broke out there, too," he continued. He and his family were sent to a camp in northern Italy that he described as "like a paradise compared to Germany" and treated rather well. While there, Bruno contracted typhoid and spent months in a hospital.

"And then the Germans took over and we were running again. A radio announcement came that all Jews had to come to the police station to identify themselves. The Catholic Church helped us, gave us false papers and some money so we could buy food. Otherwise, we wouldn't be able to survive. The bishop hid us in the convent with the nuns and they sent us to a farm in the country."

From there they went north to the city, where the Cardinal of Milan helped them with food and money. Here, Bruno met Elvira, an Italian nurse working in the underground.

When the war began, not only Jews but Catholics and Christians, anyone who opposed Hitler's politics was picked up, Bruno explained, noting that during the holocaust three million Christians were killed in addition to the six million Jews who perished. Bruno, his mother and brother were among the fortunate. When they were in the camps, in the early days at Buchenwald, there were reprisals—he remembers when a prisoner who had killed a guard was hanged and the whole camp made to watch—but none of the atrocities such as gas chambers that came in wartime years. "Those German camps were made for this," he said of the so-called final solution.

About the loss of so many family members, the never-to-know void of what might have happened to them, he told me that "Something like this happens in every war. A war is a war. There is no good war or bad war. Atrocities happen all over."

And when it was over in 1945, "That was a feeling!" he exclaimed. "When I saw the American troops coming into Milan in front of the cathedral—that was a feeling. To be free—to have survived....People were crying....When I saw the Americans on the tanks, and the American flag, that was a feeling." He stayed in Italy with his mother and brother until 1947 and worked with Americans on the Joint Distribution Committee, an organization that helped resettle people after the war and still exists.

Elvira gave him a dog named Cora that he describes as "just a dog" with a patch on one eye, a look-alike for the RCA trademark dog. And finally, when money came for boat tickets to America, Bruno, his mother and brother sailed into Norfolk on a freighter. "We came with nothing. We were glad to save ourselves and our dog, Cora. There was no dock. They put us off in a small boat in the open sea. The dog was on land before I was," he said, explaining that Cora jumped overboard and swam ashore.

A shoemaker who speaks six languages, Bruno settled first in New York City, where he was reunited with Elvira. Later, an opportunity came to leave the city and take a job with a shoe factory in Dillsburg. "Pennsylvania, I like," smiled Elvira. "Brooklyn, I don't like." After a time, the Dillsburg factory was sold and the two went to work at a Gettysburg shoe factory until it, too, closed and they retired.

Retirement is peaceful. The two return to Milan occasionally to visit Elvira's nieces and nephews. They take in a soccer game now and then, traveling to Harrisburg or Washington, D.C., to watch the sport.

The only tangible evidence of their nightmare years lies quietly tucked away. It is a grayed, coarse piece of cloth on which Bruno's concentration camp number was stenciled. Number 9990. "I smuggled it out between my fingers. If they had caught me, I would have been killed," he said.

At first glance, the Orthodox Jewish couple seemed out of place in provincial Adams County, but they were at peace here. Bruno and Elvira loved their neighbors, who respected them deeply and looked after the couple as if they were blood relatives.

Decoration Day
May 1984

My mother always called it Decoration Day. Every year on the 30th of May, we'd pack the potted geraniums in the bed of our Ford pickup along with garden tools, a shovel, and a push mower and travel to a little country churchyard in Blairsville, Pennsylvania. There all the Farleys were buried in a modest family plot dotted with fading marble markers.

"Don't step on the graves," she'd scold, flashing my adolescent memory back to tales of how grave-tramping disgruntled the dead.

"What happens, Mom?" I'd prod. "Do they really roll over in their graves? Will they come back and haunt us?

They can't FEEL anything now anyhow, can they, Mom?"

She'd come back with something like, "NO! I mean, I don't know. Of course they can't feel anything now. At least, I don't think so. Go tell your brother to stop climbing on that tombstone down there. He's going to break it. And don't tramp on the flowers!"

She would mow the long spring grass, kneel before the markers to pull the weeds away, pause and lean to wipe the engraving clean. But when she came to grandma's stone, the pause was always longer and time seemed like an envelope from which she took some never-written letters and read silently.

"What was she like, Mom?" I'd interrupt. I'd never known my Grandma Farley, for Mom was just 16 when she died.

"Oh...she was a lot like you."

After another pause, she would tell me stories about my grandmother, and I could see her playing the piano in the parlor or rolling back the carpet for dances where her Scottish friends would play the bagpipes. Every Decoration Day I'd hear again of Grandma's trips to Philadelphia by canal boat, of her dealings with the dark-eyed gypsies and her strength during the Great Depression. And there were always tales about my Grandpa, who'd lost one hand in an explosion and several of the fingers on the other catching snapping turtles but still could tie his shoes and accomplish nearly anything including tasks no ordinary man would dare to try—according to my mother.

And before the Farleys there were the Marquards and the Perchments and one American Indian, a Delaware or Cherokee, my mother would tell me as I handed her the flower pots. The wind would blow blossoms in her hair as she set the geraniums in their holes and heeled them in. We'd gather up the tools, stop for one last ceremonial look, and call my brother from a nearby tree to make the journey home.

It was a day to decorate the graves and a time to remember. Yet it wasn't till I was older that I learned officials had set aside this day after the 1865 ending of our horrific Civil War as a time to decorate the graves and honor veterans who served in it.

The day for me was not just a part of growing up but a memory to hold for that inevitable time when I'd long to discover who I was, where I'd come from, and just where on earth I might be heading. Since then, I've felt that just as much as any pharaoh's tomb, a country graveyard gives us a sense of history, of time and our niche in it. And though we may not know a single soul within the stone and wrought iron fences, their tranquility quenches that in us that begs to make some sense of life.

Near my present house are two old graveyards where in spring wild flowers and lilies bloom next to the long ago names of Lovina, Emeline and Isebella. We look at the old inscriptions and the morning news somehow doesn't seem so menacing. Here lies a young wife who may have died in childbirth. Across the way, a tiny sculptured lamb on flat, white marble reads: "In memory of our Willie."

In another plot are two matched head and foot stones, a husband and wife who lived to old age in the early 1800s. Women sometimes were called their husband's consorts then. How romantic this seems in those hard times. Here lies Rachel, consort of William Thompson, cut down in 1816, her 39th year. Atop her narrow marker is carved a chopped-off tree, its branches lying on the ground under the light of a crescent moon.

Nearby, the memory of 25-year-old George Dicks is etched on a hard black onyx-like stone: "Deth sezed this youth away soon in his blooming years to mouder in this clay unto my celestial Judge appears." The great monument of an Englishman who lived in Philadelphia tells us he died while visiting here.

And in another still, lies Samuel Hodge who, legend has it, lifted a great barrel full of cider to his shoulder and drank from the bunghole to show his strength and, thus, avoid a fight. His birth date unknown, he died March 17, 1783. "The strongest man that ever lived on earth at last did quietly yield up his breath. This fate is sore to all, to you and I. Come then prepare for death before you die," his epitaph warns.

Yet, on many lichen-crusted stones the rising sun peeks over a hill with still-bright hope and light. We think of this giant man and all the others—men and women just like us from another time and place who laughed and cried and pondered what their future held—and Decoration Day is again a time for remembering.

"I go up there and talk to those people," a friend who lives nearby once told me. "Some folks probably think I'm crazy."

The exact locations of these graveyards were omitted due to vandalism that occurs, even in such consecrated places as Gettysburg National Military Park

A Light for Peace
July 1988

Harrison Fair was a boy of 12 on July 3, 1938, when an aunt drove him and the rest of his family to Gettysburg for the dedication of the Eternal Light Peace Memorial. They went in her Hupmobile. Harrison's wife, Marvel, was there with her mother and father and eight brothers and sisters, though she didn't know her future husband. She was 11 years old.

The nearly 2,000 Civil War veterans who were encamped along the Mummasburg Road near the memorial were an average age of 94. "They had long beards," Harrison remembers. "It was the first time I ever saw a wooden leg."

The old vets had come here for a last reunion and to mark the 75th anniversary of the Battle of Gettysburg. Two of them, one Union and one Confederate—George N. Lockwood in Blue, and Absalom G. Harris in Gray—would unveil the Peace Light memorial, a long-awaited symbol of unity among men who'd fought brother against brother, butchering each other for honor's sake.

During the first three days of July 1863, the unassuming town of Gettysburg became a place of courage and carnage. In one hour on July 3 alone, 10,000 men were wounded or killed at Pickett's Charge. The Battle of Gettysburg marked the turning point of the Civil War and earned the little town a place in history.

Since those three awful days, Gettysburg has been crowded with visitors. First were the families coming to claim their wounded or bury their dead. Next came the tourists. Every summer tourists now jam the national military park here. All in all they're friendly folks who boost the local economy even though they snarl traffic, crowd restaurants and make Gettysburg a place the locals would just as soon avoid. This summer, the 125th anniversary of the great end-all bloody battle, there will be more tourists than ever before, all coming to see history remade.

Harrison Fair grew up in these parts, 15 miles north of Gettysburg, near the village of Latimore. Like every other boy in these hills, he'd heard Civil War yarns all his life. His grandfather walked the battlefield after those gruesome days in 1863. The Fair family was Republican when the Peace Light flame was first ignited in 1938. They weren't much interested in going all the way to Gettysburg to hear a Democrat, President Franklin D. Roosevelt, dedicate the memorial. But Harrison's aunt talked them into it, he recalls, because "It was a time in history."

Gettysburg is again having its time in history, as tens of thousands swarm here for re-enactments of the battle and the rededication of the peace memorial. The last Civil War veteran is long gone. But this summer brigades of re-enactors are marching through town in itchy woolen clothing, shooting cannons and clashing sabers. Everything is authentic, down to the braid and buttons, the black powder smoke, the fifes and drums. Artillery roars. Men moan. But now, nobody dies.

A friend of mine who teaches foreign boys at a private high school recently took her students to see the Eternal Light Peace Memorial. "What's the purpose of this thing?" asked a boy from Panama.

My friend the teacher said she guessed it was that all those years ago people in this country looked at one another and said we shouldn't fight, brother against brother, father against son, killing each other. The boy shook his head. Yes, he could understand, he said, being from Panama. At her school, my friend tells me, are other Panamanian boys sent here to avoid the military draft.

"Peace Eternal in a Nation United," read the words carved at the base of the monument. Its flame was extinguished during the oil shortage of 1974 and replaced by an energy-efficient but uninspiring electric light. Now the gas burner has been brought out of retirement and will glow again—this time for peace among nations.

As a child, Harrison Fair didn't understand all the fuss over the limestone and granite monument: after all, the nation was at peace then. He never imagined that in six short years he'd be training in B-17 bombers to fight in World War II.

203

Second Thoughts
June 1994

Would they make a scene? Turn away? Raise their voices and ask me to leave?

I'd tried getting in touch with him once 12 years earlier when our older son was experiencing blinding headaches. Just wanted some medical history, I told him. My intention wasn't to intrude in his life. I wished to meet him just this once to learn about my paternal family and, if appropriate, make my peace. No, he said. He didn't think it was a good idea.

This time, he couldn't refuse.

"I've had second thoughts about this, but I decided I'd better tell you," my mother said into the telephone. My biological father had passed away.

They'd married when she was just 16, had me seven years later and began to quarrel. He cheated on her, mistreated her, she said, and she left. She told him she never wanted to see him again, and he took her at her word. She remarried but never really got over the hurt.

Now I was on my way across the state from Adams to Westmoreland County to look into a coffin and see my father for the first time I could remember.

"Why am I doing this?" I asked my husband, tasting again the bitterness of rejection I thought I'd put away all those years ago.

He looked at me and smiled, clutching my hand on his lap beneath the steering wheel. We talked about what to say and how I would introduce myself. He helped me to rehearse. I was terrified.

Three hours down the road, we stopped for lunch.

"Not going to finish your sandwich?" he pushed.

I looked at the faces of women in the restaurant. What would *they* look like, I wondered. How old would they be?

I choked back the tears and wiped my eyes. If only I'd thought to bring my makeup kit. Didn't want to arrive looking frazzled and old. I'd worn my diamonds, my pearl earrings and some new lipstick. My plan was to exude class. But the question stuck in my throat with the last bite of turkey pita.

Why?

Why not till now? I cried silently, remembering the photo I'd found in the chiffonier, tucked inside the baby book that bore my Christian name and a different surname than the one I knew then, 40 years ago at the age of 10.

"Damn you!" I shrieked in my head.

Nothing could answer the question. Nothing I would see in his coffin could fill the void a father might have occupied in my life. Nothing could warm his cold heart or open his stiff arms. My mother had always said the eyes were the windows of the soul. I could not look into the eyes of a dead man.

My loving mate looked over at me as we neared our destination. "You'll never forgive yourself if you don't try this one last time." Yet, even when we walked from the car into the funeral home, I considered turning back.

We were early, the first to sign the guest book. Out of the corner of my eye, I glimpsed his gray face, pillowed against the puffy satin.

"He looked like me," I whispered to myself. Despite the difference in years and his sickness, there was a resemblance.

We were standing hand in hand in front of the casket when they approached us from behind: "How...do we know you? Are you friends?" one of them asked, smiling politely, three attractive women with several grown children.

I couldn't look, couldn't speak. I, who have stood up

before audiences of hundreds couldn't remember what I needed, wanted, so desperately to say. Tears gurgled deep in my throat. I might as well have been paralyzed.

"She's his daughter by a previous marriage," my husband announced softly, nodding toward the coffin.

"Your sister," I choked.

One of them looked a lot like me.

From one of my half sisters I learned that few tears would be shed for Patrick Kelly. Against their mother's wishes, two of his daughters corresponded with me for a while, but we have lost touch in recent years.

A Love Story
December 1994

What were we doing, traveling over the mountain on the day after Thanksgiving? Surely we had better things to do. We might have gone Christmas shopping, but here we were hauling out the shovel, tramping through the weeds. Fuzz from desiccated wild asters clung to our sweatshirts; Spanish needles peppered our pants.

Ironically, a Red Dog beer case lay nearby; one of its amber bottles had been tossed close to his head. But he was a hound, more than twice the size of a beagle and mostly white with black spots on his head. If he'd been my dog, I would have called him Spot.

Day after day, on my way to work, I had seen him lying there by the side of the road near an access to the state forest lands. At first I thought he was sleeping, so still was he. From the road, it didn't appear as if his big, once solid body had collided with a car. On better days, he might just have been taking in the last of the autumn sun but, clearly, now he was dead.

It was the saddest sight I'd ever seen.

He had been somebody's pet, a bird dog, it appeared. Yet no one came to claim him; he just lay there in the leaves as cars drove by and hunters headed into the forest searching for small game. He'd been someone's best friend, and there he was all alone, exposed to the elements. I thought of him when it snowed Thanksgiving eve.

"What are you planning to do tomorrow?" I asked my mate when our turkey dinner was finished. Poor old Spot would never know another turkey dinner, no more table scraps, not so much as a dribble of gravy.

"Let's wait and see," he said when I pitched my idea about putting the dead hound into the ground. I couldn't do it alone, I knew. He is the shoveler in our family...for planting trees, sinking fence posts and, yes, burying farm animals and family pets. We have a graveyard up behind the barn where two of our own dogs rest, along with cats, sheep, three goats, two calves and a goose. He'd had plenty of practice, but this animal meant nothing to us and I wasn't sure he'd want to make the trip. We awoke to a bright day, sunny and brisk, a good day for a mountain drive—a good day for doing the right thing.

"I don't know...it's pretty rocky up here," he said as we topped the mountain. I hadn't thought about the geology of the area until now. "We'll do the best we can."

We pulled over into the forestland access and tramped through empty bottles of Snapple and scrunched cans of Valvoline. Funny, I thought, what you can't see from the road. The dog lay with his back feet stretched behind him, as if he were running. Maggots already had started their work.

"Good thing he was up here, where it's cold," observed my mate.

A flinty sound split the air as he put shovel to earth. Once, twice, three times he tried before hitting a soft spot between sandstone boulders. I pushed back brush and saplings to clear the area where he shoveled. Cars and trucks motored by, slowing for the switchback curve in the road. None paid any attention to what we were doing. I pulled stones from the shallow hole as he shoveled the sandy soil until he hit rock again. Then he lifted the hollow body into the ground and folded the loam over top of it.

"There," he said, smiling when it was done.

"Thanks," I offered, and we climbed in the truck. On the day after Thanksgiving, we couldn't possibly have had anything better to do.

> *When I think of what love means to me, it isn't roman-*
> *tic interludes that come to mind but an abandoned dog*
> *given a proper burial on a crisp autumn day.*

Progress Comes to Blue Berry Road
August 1997

It is a sad day. They're widening Blue Berry Road.

Yes, that's Blue Berry—two words—for, though blueberries were cultivated back this dirt and gravel byway long before the 1980s, when Pennsylvania townships received money for signage with instructions to name every road in their municipalities, it was named by someone who didn't recognize modern spellings. Around the same time, an intersecting dirt road was officially dubbed Ball [sic] Town Road after the crying children who lived in a house halfway down its length.

Oh, there is cause for modernizing Blue Berry Road, according to township employees, who say that if emergency vehicles can't get back a public road, they'll lose state funding for maintaining it. Not that anyone who lives on the unimproved portion of Blue Berry Road cares much about emergency vehicles. There's only one house back here, the old Moore place, and the present owners like their privacy. They don't want an improved road, and word has it that they're trying to get its status returned to private right-of-way.

The real residents along this dirt and gravel cartway are the wildlife inhabiting acres and acres of woodland, meadow and underbrush far from the scrutiny of the main-road world. Today, I have come to visit them before they disappear.

A whole flock of goldfinches lilt about en concert in their molten-yellow plumage. Cottontails, opossums, red foxes and raccoons never have to worry they will meet their end under the wheels of speeding traffic on Blue Berry Road. An occasional muskrat lolls about with the bullfrogs at an adjacent pond and burrows holes in its breast. Fish and minnows skitter in the creek. Black snakes hang out here, too. The red-tailed hawk, jays, robins, mockingbirds, flickers, titmice, chickadees, several species of sparrows and woodpeckers, cardinals by the score, and crows also call these woods their home, to say nothing of the white-tailed deer.

At the start of the lane stands an old red oak with a trunk at least four and a half feet in diameter; one huge limb was cut off some time ago and still lies in pieces where it fell alongside the road. This is where the blight begins.

Where maples, beech and tulip poplars once enfolded the road in a many-shaded emerald cloak, the light of day now shines harshly through, illuminating roots and logs, bulldozed piles of earth, rock and brush, and wrenched evergreen limbs. The sad, sweet smell of bruised and broken trees fills the air. The start of a brook I photographed, silver-plated with ice one winter, has disappeared under dozer tracks.

My husband tells me he drove back here not long ago

to see signs, Burma Shave style, on the trees apparently marked for cutting: "Anyone—can build—a road—but only God—can make a tree." The new owner is holding out for now, it seems. A kind of storybook cottage, this centuries-old house, restored in the 1950s and remodeled true to period in the 1980s, was built around an historic stone dwelling. Everyone in the neighborhood looks upon it and Blue Berry Road with a sense of pride and ownership, as if this hidden place were at once a community and a personal treasure, rewarding us with a sense of innocence and coexistence with nature.

This is where we walked with our children or brought special friends. We never drove the road unless it was an absolute necessity. In winter, it was a perfect place for cross-country skiing or tobogganing. And even when life moved too fast for us to make time for walks, we felt reassured just knowing it was there—something magical and good.

Now it is bare, exposed.

The hemlocks, cedars and pines along the widened right-of-way...what will happen to them? How will the bottomland at the bend in the road be changed? What is to become of the daisies and goldenrod in the meadow and the speedwell near the marsh?

"It's a regular boulevard, a race track," my mate observes sourly as we walk to the end of the road where raspberry canes and mulitflora roses used to grab our fenders as we drove by ever so slowly. A faded "posted" sign hangs, lopsided, from a tree. As we turn and climb back out the quarter mile of despoiled scenery, a rustling of branches signals deer up ahead. First one and then another cinnamon yearling tiptoes out onto the new gravel to stop and examine us as if *they* were out perusing the wildlife of Blue Berry Road. They sniff the disturbed ground, and we wonder if they know how life will change.

In a little while, a white pickup truck comes to a slow stop next to us. One of our neighbors, a young man who's lived here all his life pulls up and shakes his head. "It's a shame," he says and drives away.

"Listen," I whisper to my mate...The bullfrog croaks goodbye, unaware that his home will soon be accessible to emergency vehicles.

Carolyn "Lee" Moore called out to invite me and our sons inside her house as we walked Blue Berry Road one day soon after we moved to our farm. "Would you like a piece of elderberry pie?" she asked, with no regard for the potentially disastrous consequences of blue-black berries in the hands of two little boys sitting on the oriental carpet she and her husband had brought home during the 1920s. They told us stories of those tumultuous times when Herbert served as an Army veterinarian, gathering wild horses from the north of China. They welcomed John, too, and offered us friendship, kindness and life lessons in patience and grace. The Moores died, one right after the other, about 20 years ago."I think I hear him walking behind me," Lee commented just after Herbert's passing. He'd raised show rabbits in his little barn along Blue Berry Road. It was here that years later a subsequent owner thought he saw a white-haired man in bib overalls—Herbert's favored work clothes— hanging about.

Glenn
July 1998

They asked my stepfather what year it was, and he didn't know.

211

They asked him what month it was, and he didn't know.

They asked him his name. And, that, he knew.

He recalled details about his World War II military service for them: how the "Japs" bombarded the destroyer he was on right in Pearl Harbor; how he fought the enemy again on the island of Saipan, the meanest battleground in the South Pacific. But he couldn't remember that Franklin Roosevelt was president then, and he didn't know who was president today. And he couldn't tell them what day of the week it was.

Those war years were probably the best time of Glenn Scofield's life. He got blown off his gun at Pearl Harbor that fateful December 12, but his injuries weren't severe and he was back on duty before long. Saipan was cruel, and he was lucky to get out alive.

He had friends then. He brought home pictures of them: bare-chested young Army buddies, who all seemed to look like Frank Sinatra; dark-skinned, doe-eyed island girls in grass skirts and leis; enlisted men and officers in uniforms just like his, all lined up for their platoon photograph.

It must have been good to get away from the overbearing sister and unhappy mother who'd dictated his every move back home in a Pennsylvania mill town. He was little more than a high school kid with a taste for Lucky Strikes when he was drafted. In the Army he developed a taste for beer. Not long after he came home, he married my mother.

When I was little, I used to snoop in the boxes stored in the den of our apartment above Ida Adams's beer garden. I'd pull out the brittle Kodak envelopes of black-and-white photos with deckle edges and puzzle at the people in the pictures. He looked happy there on that hot, white sand. And I wondered if he was happy when he brought home the wide, white obi-like belt on which some Japanese mother had embroidered French knots for every friend of her soldier son.

He wasn't happy in my childhood unless you counted those rare occasions when Boots, the cat, had jumped on his shoulder as he made himself a sandwich after walking home from second shift at the mill. Somehow, I couldn't connect the smiling young man in the photos with the Army private who'd taken the friendship belt from the enemy soldier he'd killed or the man who'd become my stepfather and now sat in my mother's kitchen eating a Limburger sandwich and drinking Black Label beer. It didn't occur to me until much later that maybe he couldn't either. Maybe that's why he seemed stuck in the bottom of the ever-present bottle.

Before long, my baby brother was born, and we moved from the second-floor city apartment to a rental house in the country. It was a good growing-up for us; we neither knew nor cared that we were only half brother and sister. Our mother showed us how to climb trees, find May apples and make mud pies. We sledded, ran from the neighbor's bull and played teepee under a card table draped with blankets. Our father sat in the background, an amber bottle in his hand.

We moved again, this time to a place of our own—12 acres purchased with money from Grandpap's will, on which we built the basement for a little hip-roofed house that the plans pictured as the ideal single-family dwelling of the Fifties. We moved into the basement, waiting for the day when we'd saved enough to get a loan from the bank. And the years passed. In 1960 when I graduated from high school, they put up the shell, got it under roof and laid the brick. Our father spent my graduation night at Denny's Tavern and refused to cosign as a guarantor for my college loans. By 1964, when I graduated from college, they had plumbed and plastered and almost finished the tidy little dwelling. My mother and brother attended my college graduation.

In the subsequent years, I married, my brother went away to college, and the bank foreclosed on the house and land after our father drank away the money Mom had saved to pay the taxes. Our parents separated.

Time passed, and my bitterness subsided. Dad had gone away several times to dry out at facilities for alcoholics, and occasionally we met for family gatherings. Mostly due to the havoc wreaked by alcohol on his organs, Dad's health failed. He didn't have much to say unless you asked him about his war experiences, and even then he seemed only partially with us, his speech drifting midsentence. The light of his life was a neighbor's cat that dropped by his house for treats.

Years passed, and he nearly died twice from a bleeding ulcer. Later, he developed an aneurysm. Last year, he barely survived a heart attack, and when he came home from the hospital, he behaved more strangely than ever. He refused to see the visiting nurse, turned away the cleaning lady, and ate candy instead of taking his medication. His weight dropped drastically to below 100 pounds.

My brother and mother had to lie about where he was going to get him to the Veterans Administration hospital, and he was outraged when he discovered their intentions. "I could ask you a bunch of questions about presidents," he told the doctor, "and I'll bet you wouldn't be able to answer them either."

Ours was the classic alcoholic's family with arguments routinely erupting between my stepfather and me at the dinner table. As I grow older, I think about Glenn's life and am more generous than I was inclined to be as a teenager.

Neighborhood Tradition Lost
May 1999

Hazel was angry with me, and she had every right to be. You see, I had neglected my part in taking up the collection.

She hadn't even asked me to do it in so many words. When I heard the news about our kind and quiet friend who'd passed away, I volunteered. It wasn't much to do, after all. I would canvass just the few families at the end of the road who weren't at home when she and her niece had made their visits the day before.

But I went out with a friend the next day and forgot to do it until it was too late. The following day when I got home from work, late as usual, Hazel was waiting for me. She needed to record all the names of contributors before the funeral the following morning, and here I was just getting home by the time most folks were doing their dinner dishes. I'd go this evening, I offered weakly. She'd do it herself, Hazel said.

It was clear, I'd greatly disappointed her by failing to fulfill my responsibilities, and it now appears that the tradition of taking up a collection, when one of our small number passes on, has died. To tell the truth, I'd all but forgotten about the custom that was introduced to me by Hazel's brother, Paul, some 25 years before.

In the latter half of those years, I'd gone back to work full-time; but when we first moved to the country, I was one of the few young adults who stayed at home during the day. Paul, or "Pap" as every younger person—and they were mostly all younger than he—called him, knocked at my back door carrying a zippered money pocket like the kind people used for putting cash in the night deposit at the bank and an envelope on which a few names were written. He gave me the news of the person who'd just

215

died and told me it was customary hereabouts for the neighbors to take up a collection, to buy flowers if appropriate, and give the remaining funds to the family of the deceased.

I signed my name to the envelope, and Pap pointedly looked away so as not to glimpse the amount of money I placed in the pouch. Later, when the old man enlisted me to help in these collections, I realized a kind of belonging and fitting in to the community that came to the bearer of the sad news and the carrier of the pouch.

As near as I can figure, this practice served two purposes: to inform neighbors who might not otherwise know of the passing of one of their number, and to care for families under duress. In earlier times—when entertainment amounted to walking up Dickey's Hill in search of wildflowers, and what passed for a media presentation was the showing of lantern slides on a neighbor's parlor wall—it was customary to reach out to those in need.

If a neighbor's child strayed from the path, people noticed and felt duty-bound to set him straight. Should a young woman take up with a fast crowd, she would be pulled aside and cautioned about the fragility of her reputation. When a couple courted and married, it was a neighborhood event, complete with serenading the newlyweds on their wedding night. And if a local family fell on sickness or hard times, their neighbors saw to it that they had food and shelter.

Fortunately, there was no such thing as anonymity in those days. You couldn't fade into the background. Your neighbors knew when you were born, they took note of how you lived, and they marked the circumstances of your passing. The collection at someone's death wasn't a form of charity; it was a gesture of respect for the human condition and an outward demonstration of the biblical advice to "love thy neighbor."

Not long after I started back to work, a very close friend who lived just over the hill passed away. This was a neighbor who'd taken me under her wing soon after we moved to the country, stopping me as I walked the dirt road past her house with our two little boys, passing the time of day, and offering us a piece of elderberry pie. I remember the sinking feeling I experienced when I heard about her death—the recognition that I'd just given up something irreplaceable for a career with a regular paycheck. I had that feeling again on Saturday.

My neighbor died and I wasn't even aware that he'd been sick. And, to make matters worse, I'd forgotten to do my neighborly duty.

Nearly two centuries ago, the poet Wordsworth must have had these same emotions when he wrote:
"The world is too much with us; late and soon,/Getting and spending, we lay waste our powers;/Little we see in Nature that is ours."

There are those who would disagree with Wordsworth, and many who might think my neighborhood hopelessly backward. I felt that way myself when we first moved here, but it is only now when I see the imminent demise of the old ways that I realize what I have lost.

I wonder who will take up the collection for humankind.

The traditional sympathy offering has ceased; as a result, we sometimes only learn of a neighbor's death months after the fact.

Summer Slips Away
November 2002

I have left a window open for you.
You went away suddenly and irrevocably, without so

much as an Indian summer's goodbye kiss. Yet I crave your return.

I'd grown accustomed to your warm breath ruffling my curtains and wafting over my body at night. Accustomed to my easy awakenings in your blush.

Now when I haul myself out for morning walks with the dogs, my breath hangs white in the cold air. Gone is the incredible lightness of summer being. Gone with the robins, the butterflies, the crickets and katydids. Holed up with the cicadas. Acquiring a heavy winter coat, as the mare that once stood out in the pasture did, this time of year.

On a rare sunny afternoon, a lethargic, Johnny-come-lately grasshopper stirs first one right-angle leg and then the other in the detritus of my garden as if his feet are stuck in molasses.

Last weekend, I brought my plants in from the deck. The palm tree will have to be repotted, and has grown so tall it might not fit into our sunroom—except that the plant has developed a dowager's hump on the longer of her two trunks. As I struggle to squeeze the foliage into the peak of our vaulted ceiling, I think how my trunk will no doubt mimic the palm's in later years. I take solace in the fact that the crook in her back will help her to accommodate this space a wee bit longer.

Each year I try to forestall your goodbye for as long as possible. This year, as most, I have planted hardy purple ornamental cabbage and kale along with sky-blue and sun-yellow pansies. Hoping to spare them the killing frost, I took cuttings of the dragon-wing begonias and put them in a rooting mix before I dug their still-red blooms out of the pots outside my windows. In coming weeks, I will put to bed the tender perennials and tuck the pot of hens 'n' chicks, a few geraniums, a dozen small potted evergreens, and other potential survivors under a blanket of leaves on the leeward side of the house.

High on a tree trunk outside my window, my husband has hung a terra-cotta sunburst to supplant the real Sol, whose seldom-seen face now will commence its decline in the sky on its way to winter solstice.

Oh, how I yearn for a day of making hay while the sun shines, for a barefoot walk in grass dripping with morning dew, for the soft beating of hummingbird wings, for a lazy afternoon of reading in the hammock when it's too hot to do anything else. "We need to take that hammock in," I said to my mate not long ago. To which he nodded in agreement and reluctantly added it to the messy annual cleaning of our wood stove and chimney on our to-do list. Neither has been accomplished, and so the hammock now drips, graying with wet maple leaves, and the old walk-in fireplace remains closed and quiet without so much as a sweeping out of the few unfortunate starlings that surely lie, cold and stiff, in the stove's firebox.

"But I like the change of seasons," I often respond to those who suggest that, now retired from workaday life, we might move south for the winters. Today is raw with rain and sleet, and I momentarily doubt the wisdom of my remarks.

Still, you've left mementos for me: the variegated yellow-crimson of a sugar maple out back, five-leafed flames of Virginia creeper gaffed up the weathered side of the barn, a transient bluebird stopping briefly at our feeder, and the tenacious glow of the beech trees' dried yellow leaves that will light our woods in winter. For these, though they be mere crumbs of your presence, I am thankful.

For you, I've left a bedroom window halfway open—just in case you want to drop by one more time before you go.

My earlier-born friends used to comment that summers passed more quickly as they grew older; in this, my 66th year, I completely understand.

A Death in the Family
April 2004

When the phone jars you to consciousness in the wee hours of the morning, you know it's not good. Her passing brought to mind James Agee's *A Death in the Family*, a classic novel that first described to me how a death changes everything and yet allows so much to remain the same.

"I'm sure it was a life well-lived and shared with family and friends," a woman I know said recently, expressing her sympathy at my mother-in-law's passing. I thanked her and thought of the enigmatic matriarch.

It had been a long time since my husband and I stood in the receiving line at a viewing. Barbaric, not for us when our time comes, we'd decided about the open-casket custom. It had been years, too, since our children had seen their aunts, uncles and cousins all under the same roof. We'd forgotten what a wonderful slice of humanity walks through the funeral home doors.

I've attended some sad, sparse funerals of people who'd kept to themselves, and I worried that my mother-in-law's memorial might prove the same.

I was wrong.

Death observes no calendar, arbitrarily selecting its own inconvenient appearance date. Yet every aged great-aunt, every tottering uncle and most of their progeny took the time to pay their respects to this woman and her immediate kin. Surviving pillars of the crossroads community where she lived most of her reclusive life turned out.

They came not just to honor her but to show respect for her long-gone husband, highly regarded by his peers, and her six children, who'd come of age here. My husband and I grew up in the same locale, and so for us, it seemed more like a homecoming than a funeral, bringing back to life people we'd put away in a *Twilight Zone* of high school yearbook photos 40-some years ago. Like us, they looked the same but older:

"I'll bet you don't remember me."

"We rode the school bus together."

"You know, I had a dream about you..."

"How come you moved away?"

One by one, they offered condolences and memories of our youth, when the whole world lay ahead of us. Childhood pranks, vintage cars, high school proms, and best friends drifted across the smiles and conversations that followed each handshake.

Relatives unrecognized by our sons renewed their acquaintance, recalling them as little cherubs at their grandfather's funeral or their cousins' weddings, fleshing out the stick figures of childhood memories:

"Don't you remember Uncle Gilbert?"

"That's Uncle Lester's daughter Leslie. She's a stewardess."

"My, you're good looking boys."

"No, I'm Aunt Lorraine...Aunt Dorothy is over there!" Vignettes of family history were dusted off and embellished for us by white-haired widows and neighborhood heroes with canes and walkers. Teenaged friends of our nieces fiddled with each other's jewelry and awkwardly hustled about. Siblings hugged one another with genuine care. A baby fussed, impatient with being passed from one cousin to another.

It was an exhausting day, presided over by the deceased in this ages-old tradition. But, when all was said and done, the woman we'd come to bury had reached out in a way she could not in life and brought us together again.

Little more than a year after we buried her mother, my youngest sister-in-law was stricken with a brain aneurysm and died hours later, leaving a 19-year-old daughter and a 14-year-old son. Dumbfounded, we repeated the western Pennsylvania funeral home rituals and vowed to take nothing thereafter for granted.

Over the River
November 2004

It was a risk, taking her out on a rainy day for a trip into the past. Nostalgia in our family always is viewed through the hazy lens of what might have been, always toasted with a cup half empty. "Let's go, Mom," I said. We were taking the *Over the River and Through the Woods* trip to grandmother's place that had never been possible because my grandmother lost her farm in the late 1920s and died 10 years later.

Though she was a baby when they moved there, my now-85-year-old mother, Margaret Scofield, remembers their years on the Indiana County farm in vivid detail. Likewise, she still knows the way, via a series of twisting, turning back roads, as if she'd never left.

We have a vintage photo of her, sitting barefoot and smudge-faced on the rickety front steps of the weatherboard house. She looks about four and is holding her pet chicken as she squints for the camera.

"The house was over there," she said. "The barn was right back here...there's where the chicken house used to be." A full corncrib, tractors and equipment in various states of repair, and fresh tracks in the mud confirmed the farm's continuing, if marginal, operation. She gathered her courage and approached the door of a garage apartment on the property.

"My wife's grandfather will be back soon...he's sure to remember 'cause he's always telling us stories," a young man offered. It was raining again, and my tiny mother adjusted her plastic rain hat to better look up into his pleasant face. "You'll see his pickup—it's blue—parked right out back, here."

We drove on down the road.

"Turn here...this was Yarnicks' farm," she told me. The night of the foreclosure, her parents packed everything they could get into her dad's Model-A Ford and fled with their four children to these neighbors. Acres of greenhouse-like structures lay before us; the thriving agricultural enterprise specialized in hydroponic tomatoes and cucumbers. Again, my mother got out of the car and approached strangers with her history. A woman roughly my age summoned her brother, and together they listened raptly to my mother's memories of their Aunt Sophie and other family members now gone.

As we drove back out, a complimentary basket of tomatoes and cucumbers in the trunk, she spied the blue pickup truck and we stopped.

"Yes, yes...I do remember. My dad told me about the Farleys," the gray-haired farmer allowed. "Do you have a minute?" he asked pointing to his rancher, "I have a picture of the old house." He'd had to take the structure down a few years back, he explained.

In his kitchen, he offered up a story of several depression-era families, bilked out of their investments in the 130-acre farm by the same ruthless speculator who'd sold it to them, employing the same scheme time after time. He particularly remembered the Farleys, who'd owned the place just before his folks. He recounted how the unscrupulous man convinced my mother's parents, who had the money to pay for the land in full, to put off paying the balance and use their cash in hand for a team of mules and equipment he said they'd need to farm. In the fifth year, when the final payment was due, farming was bad and they'd had a hard go of it. Not to worry, the man said, he didn't need the money and wouldn't mind their paying later. However, the day after their payment was due, he arrived with the sheriff to foreclose.

Her parents came back several years later to visit, he told my mother: "Mrs. Farley sat in our kitchen and cried." The swindler would have cheated his parents in exactly the same way, but this time he died on the very day he foreclosed, and the court gave them a year to come up with their final payment.

"Oh, thank you," my mother said when he'd finished the story. "I never knew why they lost the farm. You've given me a gift."

On the way home, we stopped for dinner at a restaurant named Granny's Place. "I'm so glad we came today," she told me with a smile.

It is ironic that my mother, who is nearly 90, repeated her own mother's experience, losing her little farm to foreclosure in the 1960s. During what some now are calling the Great Recession of 2009, we are again glimpsing some of the hard times and charlatan behaviors that emerged during the Great Depression.

Hat Ladies
April 2004

Mary Prosser and her sister, Jean Hess, are proof that it doesn't take a lot of money to make a difference in the lives of others.

They are the Hat Ladies.

Prosser, who retired some time ago from her job at the Book-of-the Month Club, will turn 81 in May. She had been knotting comforters for a local church mission project but was looking for something different. "So we got out of the blanket business and started this," she told me, holding up a ski hat. Besides, she likes crocheting. When her children fuss at her for working so hard, she tells them, "It's either crochet or go crazy."

Hess, retired after 37 and a half years with Bell Telephone, is 76 and lives just down the road from her sister in Latimore Township, Adams County.

To date, the two have crocheted more than 468 ski hats, according to Prosser's record book, in which she has logged the number of hats they've put out each year since 2001. At first, the hats were distributed along with sweaters, scarves, and blankets made by women of the Chestnut Grove Lutheran Church in a project organized by Shirley Smith, a friend of Hess's. Prosser attends the Zwingli Church in East Berlin.

The hats went to Children's Aid Society in New Oxford, Survivors Inc. in Gettysburg, and Tender Care Pregnancy Centers in Gettysburg, Hanover and Camp Hill. Later, some made their way to the Lutheran church's clothing pantry in York Springs.

When a McSherrystown high school teacher, Mary Furlong, volunteered to help set up schools in Africa, the sisters became aware of the need for warm clothing among children in Zambia during our summer, which is their winter. Most of the children have lost their parents to AIDS, and the schools are rapidly becoming like orphanages. Furlong wrote about their poverty in letters to people back home, noting that winter was coming. Now, many of the hats go to Africa, and the Hat Ladies' reputation has grown so that each new class coming to the Zambian schools wants to know when they'll be getting their hats.

"I want you to know, she does most of the crocheting," Hess says, crediting her sister, although she crochets

225

some and helps Prosser to do the pom-poms, which require two pairs of hands. In the summer, when it's too hot to be doing much else, Prosser sits on her front porch, crocheting hats.

"She likes to keep her hands busy," Shirley Smith later commented about Prosser. "Here we are, halfway around the world, and these African kids are getting the feeling, 'Somebody cares about me...somebody made this for me,' from this little old lady in the boondocks."

Prosser told me, "I love the different colors of yarn." She's even more thrilled by the diversity of the recipients. Though she may never get to Africa, her fondest wish is to see, "one of our hats coming down the street" on a child.

When I asked where they get their materials, Hess grinned and said, "I was waiting for you to ask that." Some of the yarn is donated, Prosser buys some with 40% off coupons at a local craft store, and some is bought at auctions; however, the sisters get most of it at yard sales. "I can't wait for the yard sales to start up again," Hess chuckled, suggesting that her sister show me her stash.

"You show her," Prosser reluctantly allowed, and Hess took me into a spare room, where plastic bins and cardboard boxes overflowed with skein upon skein, making a jumbled yarn rainbow. In the living room, hats of sage green, paprika, peach, purple and cocoa brown lay about in various stages of completion.

"I think the red ones are exceptionally pretty," Prosser piped.

Mary Furlong wrote back from Zambia that it takes the children in one of the bush schools six hours to walk to the nearest town, that there are no motor vehicles and just one bicycle in their village.

This time, 81 of the 105 hats crocheted so far this year will travel to Africa. The Hat Ladies have received a Zambian wall hanging and photographs of the children—

black-skinned faces smiling out from under hand-cro-
cheted toppers of green, pink, aqua, lavender, red and
blue.

*"Hat Ladies" never appeared in the most widely cir-
culated newspaper I wrote for; it was, in retrospect,
the catalyst for my column's eventual retirement. A
few years earlier I'd sat down with my editors at
this newspaper, which had been bought by a large
national publishing company. "We're trying to ap-
peal to a younger audience," they announced, ad-
vising I keep that perspective in mind when
choosing column subjects. The Prosser sisters
waited, week after week. Though their story did
publish in a small-town newspaper that had faithfully printed my column since its early days, it was
simply lost in the shuffle at the bigger organ, sig-
naling the end of an era for me. Now it seems the
end of an era for newspapers as many downsize in
their battle with the Internet.*

*The week of her death in October 2006, her sister,
Jean, sent the last of Mary Prosser's hand-cro-
cheted hats to Ingathering Sunday at the Lutheran
Church in York Springs. She never traveled to
Africa in person, but hundreds of Prosser's hand-
crocheted hats are there, warming Zambian bush
children who have no parents to care for them. I'm
told the orphans at the school include the hat ladies
in their prayers every day.*

I retired my column in May 2005.

Epilogue

⚭

The summer of 2005 brought a bumper crop of tomatoes to my garden, but when John and I prepared to go away on vacation, I panicked about who would pick and use them. Our friends said they had plenty, thank you, and our kids had never developed a taste for the juicy red fruit. Who would want my tomatoes?

I hadn't visited Hazel Johnson since writing a column about her some years back, but I knew that at age 94 she'd had to give up her garden. I called, and Hazel came even though she wasn't really up to it, as she'd recently injured a leg when she fell in her basement. She enlisted her nieces to help her harvest and can the tomatoes that hot early September. My surplus produce was a blessing in disguise. They got the tomatoes; I got reacquainted with a local gem.

"Tuh-may-tuhs," Hazel pronounced the word, *tomatoes*. I loved to hear her say that one of her favorite things to eat was stuffed green peppers with "tuh-may-tuh" gravy, and one evening after we returned from our trip, I made this supper meal and took her a serving with a side of mashed potatoes. We talked, and she told me that, at the urging of her only surviving sister, she was moving to Whispering Pines, an assisted-living facility nearby in York Springs. "Just for the winter," was how she'd convinced herself, assuring me she'd come back for good in the spring to the house she'd rented from her nephews for the past 30-some years.

"What are you doing for Thanksgiving?" I ventured.

"Oh, I guess just being thankful," she said.

When I asked if she'd want to be thankful with us, she agreed to share our turkey dinner and on Thanksgiving Day regaled my family with stories about country life in the old days.

"Just like *Fried Green Tomatoes*," was how our younger son's girlfriend put it.

It became evident that her family, the Bupp clan, also thought it best for Hazel to move. Not long after she'd reluctantly gone to "the home" in York Springs, her sister, whom she'd named as her power of attorney, began cleaning out the old brick house. Despite an early spell of searing cold weather, Hazel coaxed people to bring her out to the farm on weekends, and she set about frantically sorting and boxing nearly a century's worth of possessions. Living as close to the bone as she did, Hazel wasted nothing and saved everything. A gift of a seedling might be planted for one of her friends in a 15-year-old can, a plate was returned in a recycled bread bag. It was a lot to sort through, and the job took its toll. Hazel suffered a heart attack late one night at Whispering Pines and lasted only a few days at the same local hospital where she'd earned her living as a maid until her retirement.

One of the home's requirements was that residents make their funeral plans, and Hazel had planned well. She'd wanted to will her body to science, but the funeral director persuaded her that, given her age, her body might well have outlived its usefulness to science. She'd decided on this not just out of a sense of duty but also as a means of economizing on her final expenses, having already determined that "anything that's left" of her estate would go to a Christian home for troubled youth in upstate New York. She settled for cremation because it cost less.

Our entire family attended Hazel's funeral service and

observed that it was just the way she wanted it. Her new pastor read the eulogy; her former pastor sang an old-time hymn, and her niece, Josephine, played more hymns on a push-button accordion.

The day after her death, just a week before Christmas, I was talking to a friend about Hazel's upcoming sendoff when the telephone went dead. After a few failed attempts at raising a dial tone, I looked out our kitchen window to see John's workshop in flames. At about the same time, he heard someone yelling outside and found a woman pulled off the road and into our driveway. On her cell phone, she was dialing 911.

By the time we discovered the fire, it was too late to do anything but get our vehicles parked in the driveway out of harm's way before the fire trucks arrived.

Less than 10 years old, the building was the newest structure on the farm, a large board-and-batten garage that my husband and our sons had built together. After decades of lying on the ground in snow and rain, he'd finally had a warm, comfortable place to work on his vehicles and, more recently, to house his part-time business of rebuilding sailboat engines. It contained a lifetime of tools John had collected himself or inherited from his father. When the firemen finally left that day, all that remained was a black heap and hardened puddles of metal. My normally pragmatic mate was devastated.

This, however, wasn't the end of bad news. The day of Hazel's service, we learned that a young man we'd watched grow up, who was about to graduate with honors from Penn State, was killed in an accident on the Pennsylvania Turnpike as he drove to Philadelphia for his very first job interview. His parents, mentioned earlier in this book, are lifelong friends who'd introduced us to cross-country skiing.

We had another funeral to attend, but while Hazel's

had been a celebration of a life well lived, this one was sad beyond belief.

The following year brought many challenges as we sifted through the ashes and were ultimately cancelled by our insurance company after months of sitting on pins and needles. But not long after the New Year, one of Hazel's great-nephews, who knew I would appreciate a reminder of her, brought me a treasured memento.

A vintage half-gallon Atlas canning jar with a glass lid, it contains snow water that Hazel had preserved some years ago, melting and canning snow to see her through the winter months when the path from her house became too icy and treacherous for treks outdoors to the spring that was her source of drinking water. Hazel's jar of snow water now graces my kitchen counter, sparkling in the sunlight under the dusty cellar patina I am reluctant to wash from it. It prompts me to smile more often and be grateful for things that I take for granted such as running water and plumbing in my house. It reminds me of the last thing our village matriarch said to my son and his girlfriend when they took her home after our Thanksgiving dinner: "My, but didn't we have the *wonderfullest* garden this year!"

Indeed, my life in Adams County has been filled with wonder beyond anything I might have wished for when I transplanted myself into this Grandma Moses scene with such longing 30-some years ago. And if I should slip ever so slightly back into that outsider's persona, I have only to look at the reflection in Hazel's jar of snow water to know that, here, I truly belong.

Index

A-E

F-J

K-O

P-T

W-Z